MASTERING COMMUNITY ASSOCIATION MANAGEMENT: A GUIDE TO BUILDING THRIVING COMMUNITIES

RITA KHAN

MBA, CMCA, AMS, PCAM, ARM, ACOM, CPM, CAM, CAPS,
CPO, PMP, CSM, CDMP, PCM, SMS, AHWD, E-PRO

TABLE OF CONTENTS

Chapter 3: Building Strong Partnerships with the Board and Community

Chapter 4: Decoding Professional Credentials

Chapter 5: Mastering Communication in Community Management

Chapter 6: Trusting and Collaborating with Professionals

Chapter 7: Path to Effective Management

CHAPTER 1

UNDERSTANDING COMMUNITY ASSOCIATION MANAGEMENT

INTRODUCTION TO COMMUNITY ASSOCIATION MANAGEMENT

Community association management is a specialized field focused on the governance, administration, and oversight of residential communities such as homeowners associations (HOAs), condominium associations, and cooperatives. These associations are formed to manage and maintain common areas, enforce rules, and provide services that enhance the quality of life for residents. Effective management is crucial to the success of these communities, as it ensures the proper functioning of operations, maintains property values, and fosters a harmonious living environment.

Community association managers are the linchpins of this process, serving as the primary point of contact between residents, the board of directors, and service providers. Their responsibilities are broad and varied, requiring a deep understanding of governance, financial management, maintenance, and legal compliance. This chapter will explore the foundational concepts of community association management, providing a comprehensive overview of the roles and responsibilities of managers, the different types of community associations, and the legal frameworks that govern them.

TYPES OF COMMUNITY ASSOCIATIONS

Community associations are structured in various ways, depending on the type of property and the needs of the residents. The three primary types of community associations are homeowners associations (HOAs), condominium associations, and cooperatives. Each type has its unique characteristics, governance structures, and management requirements.

1. **Homeowners Associations (HOAs):**

    Homeowners associations are the most common type of community association in the United States, typically found in planned communities of single-family homes. HOAs are established to manage common areas such as parks, playgrounds, and swimming pools, and to enforce community standards and regulations. The HOA is governed by a board of directors, elected by the homeowners, who are responsible for making decisions that affect the community.

    The primary responsibilities of an HOA include:

    - **Maintenance of Common Areas:** The HOA is responsible for the upkeep of common areas, ensuring that they are safe, clean, and well-maintained. This includes tasks such as landscaping, snow removal, and repair of shared facilities.
    - **Enforcement of Rules and Regulations:** The HOA enforces the community's governing documents, which typically include covenants, conditions, and restrictions (CC&Rs). These documents outline the rules that homeowners must follow, such as architectural guidelines, noise restrictions, and pet policies.
    - **Collection of Assessments:** Homeowners in an HOA are required to pay assessments or dues, which are used to fund the maintenance of common areas and other community

expenses. The HOA is responsible for collecting these assessments and managing the association's finances.

- **Dispute Resolution:** The HOA may also play a role in resolving disputes between homeowners, particularly when it comes to issues related to compliance with community rules.

2. **Condominium Associations:**

Condominium associations are commonly found in multi-unit residential buildings, where individual units are owned by residents, but common elements such as lobbies, gyms, and exterior areas are collectively owned by the association. Like HOAs, condominium associations are governed by a board of directors, elected by the unit owners.

The responsibilities of a condominium association include:

- **Management of Common Elements:** The association is responsible for maintaining and repairing common elements, ensuring that they are safe, functional, and aesthetically pleasing. This includes areas such as the building's exterior, elevators, hallways, and shared amenities.

- **Financial Management:** The association manages the community's finances, including the collection of monthly fees from unit owners. These fees are used to cover maintenance costs, insurance, and reserves for future repairs.

- **Enforcement of Bylaws and Rules:** Condominium associations enforce the community's bylaws and rules, which govern everything from noise levels to the use of common areas. The association has the authority to impose fines and take legal action against unit owners who violate these rules.

- **Insurance and Risk Management:** The association is responsible for securing insurance coverage for the building and common elements, protecting the community from potential risks such as fire, water damage, and liability claims.

3. **Cooperatives:**

Cooperatives, or co-ops, are a less common form of community association, where residents do not own their individual units but instead own shares in a corporation that owns the entire property. The cooperative board of directors, elected by the shareholders, is responsible for the management and operation of the property.

The key responsibilities of a cooperative board include:

- **Property Management:** The cooperative is responsible for the maintenance and operation of the property, including common areas and individual units. This often involves hiring a property management company to handle day-to-day tasks such as repairs, cleaning, and security.

- **Approval of New Shareholders:** One of the unique aspects of cooperatives is that the board has the authority to approve or deny the sale of shares and the admission of new residents. This allows the board to maintain control over who lives in the community.

- **Financial Oversight:** The cooperative manages the community's finances, including the collection of monthly maintenance fees from shareholders. These fees cover the property's operating expenses, mortgage payments, and reserves for future improvements.

- **Governance and Decision-Making:** The cooperative board is responsible for making decisions on behalf of the shareholders, including setting policies, managing budgets, and overseeing major projects. The board must act in the best interests of the entire community, balancing the needs and preferences of individual shareholders with the overall well-being of the property.

ROLES AND RESPONSIBILITIES OF COMMUNITY MANAGERS

Community managers play a vital role in the success of any community association. They act as the operational arm of the board of directors, carrying out the decisions made by the board and ensuring the smooth functioning of the community. The responsibilities of a community manager are broad and can be categorized into four main areas: governance, financial management, maintenance oversight, and resident relations.

1. **Governance:**

    Community managers support the board of directors in their governance role, helping to implement policies, enforce rules, and ensure compliance with governing documents and applicable laws. Key governance responsibilities include:

    - **Board Support:** Managers assist the board by preparing meeting agendas, providing reports on community operations, and offering advice on best practices. They may also help facilitate board elections and ensure that meetings are conducted in accordance with the association's bylaws.

    - **Policy Implementation:** Managers are responsible for implementing the policies and decisions made by the board. This includes enforcing community rules, overseeing the architectural review process, and managing vendor contracts.

    - **Compliance:** Ensuring compliance with the community's governing documents and relevant laws is a critical part of a manager's role. This may involve working with legal counsel to address compliance issues, conducting regular inspections, and taking corrective action when necessary.

2. **Financial Management:**

Effective financial management is crucial to the long-term sustainability of a community association. Community managers play a key role in overseeing the association's finances, including:

- **Budgeting:** Managers work with the board to develop and manage the community's budget. This includes forecasting expenses, setting assessment levels, and ensuring that the association has adequate reserves for future repairs and capital improvements.

- **Assessment Collection:** Managers are responsible for collecting assessments from homeowners or unit owners. This includes sending out invoices, tracking payments, and managing delinquent accounts. In some cases, managers may work with legal counsel to pursue collections through liens or foreclosure.

- **Financial Reporting:** Regular financial reporting is essential for transparency and accountability. Managers prepare monthly financial statements, track expenses, and provide updates to the board on the association's financial health.

- **Reserve Fund Management:** Managers oversee the association's reserve funds, which are set aside for major repairs and replacements. This includes ensuring that the reserve fund is adequately funded and that investments are managed prudently.

3. **Maintenance Oversight:**

Maintaining the community's physical assets is one of the most visible aspects of a community manager's role. Responsibilities in this area include:

- **Maintenance Planning:** Managers develop and implement maintenance plans for the community's common areas and facilities. This includes scheduling regular inspections, coordinating repairs, and ensuring that all maintenance work is completed to a high standard.
- **Vendor Management:** Managers are responsible for selecting and managing vendors who provide services to the community, such as landscaping, snow removal, and janitorial services. This involves negotiating contracts, overseeing work, and ensuring that vendors meet their obligations.
- **Emergency Response:** In the event of an emergency, such as a fire, flood, or severe weather event, managers play a critical role in coordinating the community's response. This may involve working with emergency services, communicating with residents, and arranging for repairs.
- **Capital Improvement Projects:** Managers oversee major capital improvement projects, such as roof replacements, road resurfacing, and amenity upgrades. This includes managing the bidding process, coordinating with contractors, and ensuring that projects are completed on time and within budget.

4. **Resident Relations:**

Building strong relationships with residents is essential for maintaining a positive community atmosphere. Community managers are often the first point of contact for residents and are responsible for:

- **Communication:** Effective communication is key to keeping residents informed and engaged. Managers may use a variety of communication channels, including newsletters, emails, social media, and community meetings, to share important information and updates.

- **Resident Support:** Managers assist residents with questions, concerns, and requests related to community operations. This may include resolving disputes, processing architectural review applications, and coordinating community events.

- **Conflict Resolution:** Conflicts can arise in any community, and managers play a crucial role in resolving disputes between residents, or between residents and the board. This involves active listening, mediation, and finding solutions that align with the community's rules and policies.

- **Community Building:** Beyond administrative tasks, managers play a vital role in fostering a sense of community. This may involve organizing social events, facilitating volunteer opportunities, and encouraging resident participation in community governance.

LEGAL AND REGULATORY FRAMEWORKS

Community associations operate within a complex legal and regulatory environment, governed by a combination of federal, state, and local laws, as well as the association's governing documents. Understanding and navigating these frameworks is essential for community managers to ensure compliance and protect the association from legal risks.

1. **Governing Documents:**

    The foundation of any community association is its governing documents, which typically include the Declaration of Covenants, Conditions, and Restrictions (CC&Rs), bylaws, and rules and regulations. These documents outline the rights and responsibilities of the association, the board, and the residents. Key aspects of governing documents include:

- **CC&Rs:** The CC&Rs are the primary governing document for most community associations. They define the association's authority, outline the use restrictions for the property, and establish the process for amending the document.
- **Bylaws:** The bylaws provide the framework for the association's governance, including the structure and duties of the board of directors, the process for holding meetings and elections, and the procedures for making decisions.
- **Rules and Regulations:** These are the day-to-day operational guidelines for the community, covering issues such as noise, parking, pets, and the use of common areas. The rules and regulations must be consistent with the CC&Rs and bylaws.

2. **State and Federal Laws:**

    In addition to their governing documents, community associations must comply with a range of state and federal laws. Some of the key legal requirements include:

    - **Fair Housing Act (FHA):** The FHA prohibits discrimination in housing based on race, color, national origin, religion, sex, familial status, or disability. Community associations must ensure that their rules and practices do not violate fair housing laws.
    - **Americans with Disabilities Act (ADA):** The ADA requires community associations to provide reasonable accommodations for residents with disabilities, particularly in common areas. This may include modifying facilities or policies to ensure accessibility.
    - **State-Specific Laws:** Each state has its own set of laws governing community associations. These laws may cover issues such as assessment collection, reserve fund requirements,

board elections, and the enforcement of rules. It is essential for community managers to be familiar with the laws in their state and to seek legal advice when necessary.

- **Insurance Requirements:** State laws often require community associations to carry specific types of insurance, such as liability, property, and directors and officers (D&O) insurance. Managers must ensure that the association's insurance coverage meets legal requirements and provides adequate protection for the community.

3. **Compliance and Enforcement:**

   Ensuring compliance with governing documents and legal requirements is one of the most challenging aspects of community association management. This involves regular monitoring, enforcement of rules, and taking appropriate action when violations occur.

   - **Inspections:** Regular inspections of the community's common areas and facilities are essential for identifying potential compliance issues and ensuring that maintenance standards are met.

   - **Enforcement Procedures:** When residents violate the association's rules or governing documents, the manager must follow the association's enforcement procedures, which may include issuing warnings, imposing fines, or taking legal action.

   - **Legal Counsel:** Working with legal counsel is often necessary to navigate complex compliance issues and to ensure that the association's actions are consistent with state and federal laws. Legal counsel can also assist with drafting and amending governing documents, resolving disputes, and representing the association in legal matters.

THE CRITICAL ROLE OF COMMUNITY MANAGERS

Community managers are the backbone of any successful community association. Their role is multifaceted, requiring a balance of leadership, organization, and interpersonal skills. Managers must navigate the complexities of governance, financial management, maintenance, and resident relations while ensuring compliance with a myriad of legal and regulatory requirements.

Effective community managers are problem-solvers, capable of addressing unexpected challenges and finding solutions that align with the community's goals and values. They are also communicators, able to build trust and rapport with residents, the board, and service providers. Above all, community managers are leaders, guiding the board and the community toward a shared vision of success and harmony.

In this chapter, we have explored the foundational concepts of community association management, including the different types of associations, the roles and responsibilities of managers, and the legal frameworks that govern community operations. As we move forward in this book, we will delve deeper into the specific skills and strategies that community managers need to excel in their roles and to create thriving, well-managed communities.

CHAPTER 2

PORTFOLIO VS. ON-SITE MANAGEMENT

INTRODUCTION TO PORTFOLIO AND ON-SITE MANAGEMENT

Community association management is a dynamic field that requires flexibility, organization, and a deep understanding of the needs of each community. Managers in this industry often adopt different approaches depending on the size, location, and specific requirements of the communities they oversee. Two primary management styles are portfolio management and on-site management.

Portfolio management involves overseeing multiple properties simultaneously, often spread across different locations. The manager, known as a portfolio manager, typically handles a variety of responsibilities for each community, but may not be physically present at any one site on a daily basis. This approach allows for the efficient use of resources and standardized procedures across multiple properties.

On-site management, on the other hand, is when a manager is dedicated to a single property or community, working directly from that location. On-site managers are deeply embedded in the day-to-day operations of the community, providing immediate attention to residents' needs and being more hands-on with the maintenance and management of the property.

Both approaches have their unique advantages and challenges, and understanding these can help a manager choose the most effective strategy for their situation. This chapter will explore each management style in detail, provide practical examples, and offer guidance on how to optimize performance in both roles.

PORTFOLIO MANAGEMENT: AN OVERVIEW

Definition and Scope:

Portfolio management is a management style where a single manager is responsible for overseeing multiple communities or properties, which may be located in different geographic areas. Portfolio managers are typically employed by management companies that service various communities, and their responsibilities can range from governance and financial oversight to vendor management and resident communication.

Key Characteristics of Portfolio Management:

1. **Remote Oversight:** Portfolio managers are not stationed at any one property but instead travel between locations as needed. They often work from a central office and visit each property on a scheduled basis.

2. **Multiple Communities:** A portfolio manager might oversee a variety of properties, such as a mix of homeowners associations (HOAs), condominium associations, and even rental properties. This variety requires a broad skill set and the ability to adapt to different community needs and regulations.

3. **Standardized Procedures:** To efficiently manage multiple properties, portfolio managers often rely on standardized procedures and processes. This ensures consistency in management practices across all the communities they oversee.

4. **Time Management:** Effective time management is crucial in portfolio management. Managers must prioritize tasks, schedule

visits, and ensure that all communities receive adequate attention and support.

Benefits of Portfolio Management:

1. **Efficiency:** By managing multiple properties, portfolio managers can streamline processes, share resources, and apply best practices across different communities. This can lead to cost savings for the management company and the communities they serve.

2. **Broader Experience:** Portfolio managers gain experience across a wide range of property types and management situations, which can enhance their problem-solving abilities and overall expertise in the field.

3. **Cost-Effective:** For smaller communities or those with limited budgets, portfolio management can be a more cost-effective solution compared to on-site management. The shared management costs can reduce the financial burden on individual communities.

4. **Resource Allocation:** Portfolio managers can allocate resources more effectively, such as pooling vendors for bulk services (e.g., landscaping or maintenance) across multiple properties, leading to potential discounts and better service.

Challenges of Portfolio Management:

1. **Limited Presence:** One of the main challenges of portfolio management is the limited physical presence at each property. This can lead to delays in addressing resident concerns or resolving issues, particularly in emergencies.

2. **Workload Management:** Managing multiple properties can be overwhelming, especially during peak times or when multiple

communities require attention simultaneously. This requires excellent organizational skills and the ability to delegate tasks effectively.

3. **Communication Barriers:** Ensuring consistent and effective communication across multiple communities can be challenging. Managers must stay on top of communications from residents, boards, and vendors, which can be time-consuming.

4. **Diverse Needs:** Each community may have unique needs, governance structures, and resident expectations. Balancing these varying demands requires flexibility and a deep understanding of each community's specific requirements.

CASE STUDY: SUCCESSFUL PORTFOLIO MANAGEMENT

Consider a portfolio manager named Sarah, who oversees five communities in a suburban area. These communities range from a small condominium association with 30 units to a large HOA with over 200 single-family homes. Sarah's management approach includes:

- **Regular Scheduled Visits:** Sarah visits each community on a rotating schedule, ensuring she is present at least once a week at each property. During these visits, she meets with board members, checks on ongoing projects, and addresses resident concerns.

- **Centralized Communication System:** To manage communication efficiently, Sarah uses a centralized email system where all inquiries from residents and board members are logged and categorized. This allows her to track responses and ensure no issue is overlooked.

- **Vendor Partnerships:** Sarah has established strong relationships with a few key vendors who service all her communities.

This not only ensures consistent quality but also provides cost savings through bulk contracts.

- **Standardized Reporting:** Each month, Sarah prepares a standardized report for each community, covering financials, maintenance updates, and upcoming events. This report is shared with the board members and helps keep everyone informed and aligned.

Sarah's ability to manage her time, communicate effectively, and leverage resources across multiple communities has led to high satisfaction among residents and board members, demonstrating the effectiveness of portfolio management when done correctly.

ON-SITE MANAGEMENT: AN OVERVIEW

Definition and Scope:

On-site management is a management style where the manager is dedicated to a single property or community and works directly from that location. On-site managers are deeply involved in the day-to-day operations of the community, providing immediate attention to residents' needs, overseeing maintenance, and working closely with the board of directors.

Key Characteristics of On-Site Management:

1. **Daily Presence:** On-site managers are physically present at the property every day, allowing them to respond quickly to issues, monitor the community's condition, and engage with residents regularly.

2. **Dedicated Focus:** Unlike portfolio managers, on-site managers focus exclusively on the needs of one community. This

allows them to develop a deep understanding of the property, its residents, and its specific challenges.

3. **Hands-On Management:** On-site managers are often involved in the direct supervision of maintenance tasks, inspections, and projects. Their presence ensures that issues are addressed promptly and that the community remains well-maintained.

4. **Close Resident Interaction:** On-site managers have frequent interactions with residents, fostering strong relationships and building trust within the community. This close interaction helps in understanding residents' needs and addressing their concerns effectively.

Benefits of On-Site Management:

1. **Immediate Response:** One of the most significant advantages of on-site management is the ability to respond immediately to issues and emergencies. Whether it's a maintenance problem, a resident concern, or a security issue, the manager is on hand to address it.

2. **In-Depth Knowledge:** On-site managers develop a deep understanding of their community's unique needs, preferences, and challenges. This knowledge allows them to tailor management strategies to best serve the residents and maintain the property.

3. **Stronger Resident Relationships:** Being on-site daily allows managers to build stronger relationships with residents. These relationships can lead to higher resident satisfaction, better community engagement, and a more cohesive living environment.

4. **Enhanced Oversight:** On-site managers can closely monitor the performance of vendors, contractors, and maintenance staff, ensuring that work is completed to the highest standards and that the community is well cared for.

Challenges of On-Site Management:

1. **Scope Limitation:** Focusing on a single property can limit a manager's exposure to diverse management experiences. On-site managers may miss out on the broader knowledge and skills that come from managing multiple properties.

2. **Burnout Risk:** The constant presence and involvement in the community's daily operations can lead to burnout if not managed properly. On-site managers must find ways to balance their workload and maintain a healthy work-life balance.

3. **Resource Constraints:** Unlike portfolio managers who can pool resources across multiple properties, on-site managers may have fewer opportunities to leverage economies of scale. This can make it more challenging to negotiate vendor contracts or implement cost-saving measures.

4. **Resident Dependency:** Residents may become overly dependent on the on-site manager, expecting immediate attention to all their concerns. This can lead to an overwhelming workload if not managed carefully.

CASE STUDY: SUCCESSFUL ON-SITE MANAGEMENT

Consider an on-site manager named John, who manages a large condominium community with 150 units. John's approach to on-site management includes:

*   **Daily Walkthroughs:** Every morning, John conducts a walk-through of the property, checking for maintenance issues, safety concerns, and overall cleanliness. This proactive approach helps him identify and address problems before they escalate.

*   **Open-Door Policy:** John maintains an open-door policy, encouraging residents to drop by his office with questions,

concerns, or suggestions. This approach has helped build strong relationships and trust within the community.

- **Close Collaboration with the Board:** John works closely with the condominium association's board of directors, attending all meetings, providing detailed reports, and offering his professional recommendations on various issues. His close collaboration with the board ensures that the community's needs are met and that decisions are made in the best interest of the residents.

- **Vendor Oversight:** John personally oversees all vendor activities, from landscaping to cleaning services. He ensures that all work is completed to the highest standards and that vendors adhere to their contracts. His hands-on approach has led to a well-maintained property and high resident satisfaction.

John's commitment to his role as an on-site manager has resulted in a well-managed, cohesive community where residents feel supported and valued. His ability to address issues promptly and maintain close relationships with both the board and residents showcases the effectiveness of on-site management.

CHOOSING THE RIGHT APPROACH: PORTFOLIO VS. ON-SITE MANAGEMENT

The decision between portfolio and on-site management depends on several factors, including the size and complexity of the community, the budget, and the specific needs of the residents. Here are some considerations to help determine the best approach for a particular community:

1. **Community Size and Complexity:**
    - **Large, Complex Communities:** On-site management is often the best choice for large, complex communities with

extensive amenities and a high number of residents. The daily presence of a manager ensures that the property is well-maintained and that residents receive prompt attention.

- **Smaller Communities:** Smaller communities with fewer residents and amenities may not require a full-time on-site manager. In these cases, portfolio management can be a cost-effective solution that still provides professional oversight.

2. **Budget Constraints:**
   - **Limited Budgets:** Communities with limited budgets may benefit from portfolio management, as the shared costs can reduce the financial burden on individual properties. However, it's essential to ensure that the portfolio manager can still dedicate adequate time and resources to each community.
   - **Sufficient Budgets:** Communities with more substantial budgets may prefer on-site management, as it allows for a more personalized and responsive approach. The presence of an on-site manager can enhance resident satisfaction and ensure that the property is well cared for.

3. **Resident Expectations:**
   - **High Resident Interaction:** If residents expect frequent interaction with the manager and quick responses to their concerns, on-site management may be the better choice. The manager's daily presence can help build trust and foster a strong sense of community.
   - **Independent Residents:** In communities where residents are more independent and do not require frequent interaction with the manager, portfolio management can be an effective option. The manager can focus on overseeing the

community's operations without needing to be physically present daily.

4. **Management Company Structure:**
   - **Large Management Companies:** Larger management companies may prefer portfolio management, as it allows them to service multiple communities efficiently. They can allocate resources based on the specific needs of each property and provide managers with the support they need to succeed.
   - **Smaller Management Companies:** Smaller management companies or self-managed communities may opt for on-site management, especially if they focus on providing personalized service to their clients. The close relationship between the manager and the community can lead to higher satisfaction and better outcomes.

5. **Specific Community Needs:**
   - **Specialized Needs:** Communities with specialized needs, such as those with unique amenities or challenging maintenance requirements, may benefit from on-site management. The manager's presence ensures that these needs are addressed promptly and effectively.
   - **General Management Needs:** Communities with more general management needs, such as basic maintenance and governance, can often be managed effectively through a portfolio approach. The manager can oversee multiple properties without sacrificing the quality of service.

HYBRID MANAGEMENT MODELS:

In some cases, a hybrid model that combines elements of both portfolio and on-site management may be the most effective approach.

For example, a portfolio manager could oversee several small communities while dedicating more time to a larger, more complex property. Alternatively, a community could have an on-site manager supported by a portfolio manager who handles specific administrative tasks.

This hybrid approach allows for flexibility and can be tailored to the specific needs of the community. It ensures that each property receives the appropriate level of attention and support while optimizing the use of resources.

CASE STUDY: HYBRID MANAGEMENT MODEL

Consider a management company that oversees three communities: a large condominium complex, a mid-sized HOA, and a small gated community. The company uses a hybrid management model:

- **On-Site Manager for the Condominium:** The large condominium complex has an on-site manager who handles the day-to-day operations, resident interactions, and maintenance. This ensures that the complex's extensive amenities are well-maintained and that residents' needs are met promptly.

- **Portfolio Manager for the HOA and Gated Community:** The mid-sized HOA and the small gated community are managed by a portfolio manager who visits each property weekly. The portfolio manager oversees financial management, vendor contracts, and board communications. Since these communities have fewer amenities and lower maintenance needs, the portfolio approach works well.

- **Shared Administrative Support:** Both the on-site and portfolio managers receive administrative support from the management company's central office. This support includes handling accounts payable, preparing financial reports, and managing resident communications.

This hybrid model allows the management company to provide tailored service to each community while optimizing resources and maintaining cost-effectiveness.

EFFECTIVE STRATEGIES FOR SUCCESS IN BOTH ROLES

Regardless of whether you choose portfolio or on-site management, certain strategies can enhance your effectiveness and ensure the success of the communities you manage:

1. **Time Management:**
   - **Prioritize Tasks:** Identify the most critical tasks and focus on completing them first. This is especially important for portfolio managers who must balance the needs of multiple communities.
   - **Use Technology:** Leverage technology, such as property management software, to streamline tasks, schedule visits, and track progress. This can help you stay organized and ensure that nothing falls through the cracks.
   - **Delegate When Necessary:** Don't be afraid to delegate tasks to assistants, vendors, or board members. Delegating can free up your time to focus on higher-priority issues.

2. **Communication:**
   - **Be Proactive:** Proactively communicate with residents, board members, and vendors to keep them informed and address potential issues before they escalate.
   - **Establish Clear Channels:** Set up clear communication channels, such as email lists, online portals, or regular meetings, to ensure that everyone is on the same page.
   - **Listen Actively:** Whether you're dealing with a resident complaint or a board member's concern, active listening is key to understanding the issue and finding a solution.

3. **Resident Engagement:**
   - **Foster Relationships:** Build strong relationships with residents by being approachable, responsive, and empathetic. This is especially important for on-site managers who interact with residents daily.
   - **Encourage Participation:** Encourage residents to participate in community events, meetings, and volunteer opportunities. This can help build a sense of community and reduce conflicts.
   - **Provide Regular Updates:** Keep residents informed about community projects, events, and decisions. Regular updates can help build trust and ensure transparency.

4. **Financial Management:**
   - **Develop Accurate Budgets:** Work with the board to develop accurate and realistic budgets that account for all community expenses. This is crucial for both portfolio and on-site managers.
   - **Monitor Expenses:** Regularly review financial reports to ensure that expenses are within budget and that the community's finances are healthy.
   - **Plan for Reserves:** Ensure that the community has adequate reserves for future repairs and capital improvements. This is especially important for on-site managers who oversee large properties with significant maintenance needs.

5. **Vendor Management:**
   - **Vet Vendors Thoroughly:** Whether you're managing one property or multiple, it's important to vet vendors thoroughly before hiring them. Check references, review past work, and ensure that they have the necessary licenses and insurance.

- **Set Clear Expectations:** Establish clear expectations for quality, timelines, and communication with vendors. This can help prevent misunderstandings and ensure that work is completed to your satisfaction.
- **Monitor Performance:** Regularly monitor vendor performance and provide feedback as needed. If a vendor is not meeting expectations, address the issue promptly to avoid disruptions.

6. **Professional Development:**
   - **Stay Informed:** Keep up with industry trends, best practices, and changes in regulations. This is important for both portfolio and on-site managers to ensure that you provide the best possible service to your communities.
   - **Pursue Certifications:** Consider pursuing professional certifications to enhance your skills and credibility. We will cover certifications in Chapter 4.
   - **Network with Peers:** Networking with other community managers can provide valuable insights, support, and opportunities for professional growth.

CONCLUSION

Both portfolio and on-site management are effective approaches to community association management, each with its unique benefits and challenges. Portfolio management offers efficiency and broader experience, while on-site management provides a more personalized and hands-on approach. By understanding the differences between these management styles and applying the strategies discussed in this chapter, you can optimize your performance and ensure the success of the communities you manage.

Whether you are a portfolio manager overseeing multiple properties or an on-site manager dedicated to a single community, your role is crucial in creating thriving, well-managed communities that residents are proud to call home.

CHAPTER 3

BUILDING STRONG PARTNERSHIPS WITH THE BOARD AND COMMUNITY

INTRODUCTION TO BUILDING STRONG PARTNERSHIPS

In community association management, the success of a community largely depends on the strength of the relationships between the community manager, the board of directors, and the residents. These partnerships are the foundation of effective governance, seamless operations, and a harmonious living environment. For someone new to the community association industry, understanding how to build and maintain these partnerships is crucial. This chapter will guide you through the strategies and best practices for fostering these relationships, ensuring that all stakeholders work together toward common goals.

A strong partnership between the manager and the board of directors leads to effective decision-making, clear communication, and a united approach to community management. Similarly, engaging with the residents and creating a sense of community helps in maintaining a positive atmosphere, reducing conflicts, and enhancing overall satisfaction. Throughout this chapter, we will explore these concepts in depth, providing practical examples and actionable advice that you can apply in your role as a community manager.

UNDERSTANDING THE ROLE OF THE BOARD OF DIRECTORS

Before diving into the strategies for building partnerships, it's essential to understand the role of the board of directors in a community association. The board is typically composed of elected homeowners or unit owners who volunteer their time to oversee the governance of the community. The board's responsibilities include making decisions on behalf of the association, setting policies, approving budgets, and ensuring that the community's governing documents are followed.

Key Responsibilities of the Board of Directors:

1. **Governance:** The board is responsible for establishing and enforcing the community's rules and regulations. This includes approving amendments to governing documents, setting policies, and ensuring that the community operates within legal and regulatory frameworks.

2. **Financial Oversight:** The board oversees the association's finances, including approving budgets, managing reserves, and ensuring that assessments are collected and spent appropriately. They are also responsible for ensuring that the association remains financially solvent.

3. **Maintenance and Operations:** The board makes decisions related to the maintenance and upkeep of common areas, facilities, and amenities. This includes approving contracts with vendors, overseeing major repairs, and ensuring that the property is well-maintained.

4. **Community Engagement:** The board is the representative body for the community's residents, and it's their job to engage with homeowners and address their concerns. They also play a

role in fostering a sense of community by organizing events and encouraging resident participation.

The Manager's Role in Supporting the Board:

As a community manager, your role is to support the board in fulfilling their responsibilities. This involves providing expert advice, implementing board decisions, and ensuring that the day-to-day operations of the community run smoothly. A strong partnership with the board is essential for effective community management, as it allows you to work collaboratively to achieve the community's goals.

BUILDING A STRONG RELATIONSHIP WITH THE BOARD OF DIRECTORS

Creating a strong, collaborative relationship with the board of directors is one of the most important aspects of your role as a community manager. Here are some strategies to help you build and maintain this partnership:

1. **Establish Clear Communication Channels:**

   Effective communication is the cornerstone of any successful relationship, and this is especially true when working with the board of directors. Establishing clear communication channels ensures that information flows smoothly between you and the board, reducing misunderstandings and ensuring that everyone is on the same page.

   - **Regular Meetings:** Schedule regular meetings with the board, such as monthly board meetings or bi-weekly check-ins, to discuss ongoing projects, address concerns, and plan for future initiatives. These meetings provide an opportunity to share updates, gather feedback, and make decisions collaboratively.

- **Written Reports:** Provide the board with written reports on key aspects of community management, such as financial updates, maintenance progress, and resident issues. These reports should be clear, concise, and informative, helping the board make informed decisions.

- **Open Lines of Communication:** Encourage board members to reach out to you with questions or concerns between meetings. Whether it's via email, phone calls, or a dedicated communication platform, making yourself accessible to the board fosters trust and ensures that issues are addressed promptly.

2. **Understand Board Dynamics:**

   Each board of directors has its own dynamics, influenced by the personalities, backgrounds, and priorities of its members. Understanding these dynamics is crucial for effective collaboration. Take the time to get to know each board member, their areas of expertise, and their perspectives on community issues.

- **Active Listening:** Pay close attention to the concerns and opinions of each board member. Active listening shows respect for their input and helps you understand the group's collective priorities.

- **Respect Differences:** Recognize that board members may have differing opinions on certain issues. Your role is to facilitate productive discussions, helping the board reach consensus while respecting individual viewpoints.

- **Build Trust:** Trust is the foundation of a strong relationship with the board. Be transparent in your communications, follow through on commitments, and demonstrate your expertise and reliability. Over time, these actions will build trust and strengthen your partnership with the board.

3. **Provide Expert Guidance:**

   The board relies on you as the community manager to provide expert guidance on a wide range of issues, from legal compliance to financial management and maintenance planning. By offering informed, well-researched advice, you help the board make decisions that are in the best interest of the community.

   - **Stay Informed:** Keep yourself up-to-date on industry trends, legal developments, and best practices in community management. This knowledge enables you to provide the board with the most accurate and relevant information.

   - **Offer Solutions:** When presenting issues to the board, also provide potential solutions. This demonstrates your proactive approach and helps the board focus on decision-making rather than problem-solving.

   - **Educate the Board:** Board members may not have the same level of expertise in community management as you do. Take the time to educate them on important topics, such as budgeting, reserve studies, and vendor contracts. Providing this education empowers the board to make informed decisions.

4. **Collaborate on Decision-Making:**

   Collaboration is key to a successful partnership with the board. Rather than simply executing the board's decisions, work with them to develop strategies and solutions that benefit the entire community.

   - **Facilitate Discussions:** During board meetings, facilitate discussions in a way that encourages participation from all members. This ensures that decisions are well-rounded and take into account different perspectives.

- **Seek Consensus:** Whenever possible, aim for consensus in board decisions. Consensus-building strengthens the board's unity and ensures that decisions are more likely to be supported by the community.

- **Implement Decisions Effectively:** Once a decision has been made, it's your responsibility to implement it effectively. Keep the board informed of your progress and address any challenges that arise along the way.

5. **Address Conflicts Constructively:**

   Conflicts can arise within any board of directors, whether due to differing opinions, personality clashes, or external pressures. As a community manager, your role is to help the board navigate these conflicts constructively.

   - **Identify the Root Cause:** When a conflict arises, take the time to understand the root cause. Is it a difference in priorities, a misunderstanding, or a lack of communication? Identifying the underlying issue is the first step in resolving the conflict.

   - **Facilitate Mediation:** Act as a neutral mediator in board conflicts, helping members communicate their perspectives and find common ground. Your goal is to guide the board toward a resolution that everyone can support.

   - **Focus on Solutions:** Encourage the board to focus on finding solutions rather than dwelling on disagreements. By keeping the discussion solution-oriented, you help the board move past conflicts and continue working toward the community's goals.

ENGAGING WITH THE COMMUNITY

While building a strong partnership with the board of directors is essential, it's equally important to engage with the community's residents. A well-engaged community is more likely to be satisfied, harmonious, and actively involved in the association's activities. Here are some strategies for fostering strong relationships with residents:

1. Foster Open Communication:

Just as with the board, effective communication with residents is key to building trust and engagement. Residents need to feel that their voices are heard and that their concerns are addressed promptly.

- **Regular Updates:** Keep residents informed about community news, upcoming projects, and important decisions through regular newsletters, emails, and community meetings. Transparency in communication builds trust and reduces uncertainty.

- **Accessible Channels:** Provide multiple channels for residents to communicate with you, such as a dedicated email address, a community portal, or a suggestion box. Being accessible encourages residents to share their feedback and concerns.

- **Responsive Communication:** When residents reach out to you, respond promptly and professionally. Even if you don't have an immediate solution, acknowledging their concerns and keeping them informed of any progress demonstrates your commitment to their satisfaction.

2. Encourage Resident Participation:

Active participation from residents is vital to creating a vibrant, engaged community. By encouraging residents to get involved in community activities, meetings, and decision-making processes, you help build a sense of ownership and pride within the community.

- **Organize Community Events:** Hosting social events, workshops, and volunteer opportunities can bring residents together and foster a sense of community. Events like holiday parties, clean-up days, or educational seminars can enhance resident interaction and engagement.

- **Promote Committee Involvement:** Encourage residents to join committees that align with their interests, such as a landscaping committee, a social events committee, or a budget committee. Committee involvement gives residents a voice in specific areas of the community and helps distribute the workload.

- **Solicit Feedback:** Regularly solicit feedback from residents through surveys, polls, or suggestion boxes. Understanding residents' preferences and concerns allows you to tailor your management approach to better meet their needs.

3. **Build a Positive Community Culture:**

    Creating a positive community culture is essential for fostering harmony and reducing conflicts among residents. A community with a strong sense of identity and shared values is more likely to thrive.

    - **Promote Inclusivity:** Ensure that all residents feel welcome and valued, regardless of their background or circumstances. This includes being mindful of cultural differences, providing language support when needed, and promoting events that appeal to diverse interests.

    - **Encourage Respectful Behavior:** Set expectations for respectful behavior among residents by enforcing community rules and addressing any inappropriate conduct. Promote a culture of kindness, cooperation, and neighborliness through community guidelines and communication.

- **Celebrate Achievements:** Recognize and celebrate the achievements of residents, whether it's a well-maintained garden, a successful community event, or a resident who goes above and beyond to help others. Acknowledging positive contributions reinforces a sense of community pride.

4. **Address Resident Concerns Proactively:**

   Addressing resident concerns in a timely and effective manner is crucial for maintaining trust and satisfaction. When residents feel that their concerns are taken seriously, they are more likely to remain engaged and supportive of the community's leadership.

   - **Be Approachable:** Make it easy for residents to approach you with their concerns. Whether it's through office hours, phone calls, or informal conversations, being approachable encourages residents to voice their concerns before they escalate.

   - **Investigate Thoroughly:** When a concern is raised, investigate it thoroughly before taking action. This ensures that you have all the facts and can make an informed decision.

   - **Communicate Your Actions:** After addressing a concern, communicate the actions you've taken to the resident(s) involved. This transparency reassures residents that their concerns are being handled and shows your commitment to their well-being.

5. **Conflict Resolution Among Residents:**

   Conflicts among residents are inevitable in any community, but how they are handled can significantly impact the overall atmosphere. As a community manager, you play a key role in mediating and resolving conflicts to maintain peace and harmony.

- **Remain Neutral:** When mediating conflicts between residents, it's important to remain neutral and avoid taking sides. Your role is to facilitate a fair and respectful discussion that allows both parties to express their views.

- **Encourage Direct Communication:** Often, conflicts can be resolved by encouraging residents to communicate directly with each other in a respectful manner. Facilitate this communication if needed, and help both parties find common ground.

- **Apply the Rules Consistently:** When a conflict involves a violation of community rules, apply the rules consistently and fairly. This not only resolves the conflict but also reinforces the importance of adhering to the community's guidelines.

CASE STUDY: BUILDING A STRONG RESIDENT-MANAGER RELATIONSHIP

Let's consider a real-life example of how strong resident-manager relationships can positively impact a community:

Sierra is a community manager for a mid-sized homeowners association with 100 homes. When she first took on the role, she noticed that many residents felt disconnected from the board and management, leading to low participation in community events and frequent complaints.

To address this, Sierra implemented the following strategies:

- **Weekly Office Hours:** Sierra established weekly office hours where residents could drop by to discuss any issues or simply chat about the community. This made her more accessible and allowed her to build rapport with residents.

- **Monthly Newsletters:** She introduced a monthly newsletter that highlighted community news and upcoming events and featured profiles of residents who made positive contributions to the community. The newsletter helped improve communication and fostered a sense of community.

- **Community Events:** Sierra organized a series of events, including a summer barbecue, a holiday decorating contest, and a gardening workshop. These events brought residents together, encouraged participation, and strengthened community bonds.
- **Resident Surveys:** She conducted a survey to gather feedback on the community's rules and amenities. Based on the results, Sierra worked with the board to implement changes that reflected residents' preferences, such as adjusting pool hours and updating the playground.

As a result of these efforts, resident participation in community events increased, complaints decreased, and overall satisfaction with the management improved. Sierra's proactive approach to building relationships and engaging residents transformed the community into a more cohesive and vibrant neighborhood.

COLLABORATIVE DECISION-MAKING

Collaborative decision-making is a key component of effective community management. It involves working together with the board of directors, residents, and other stakeholders to make decisions that benefit the entire community. Here's how to foster a collaborative decision-making process:

1. **Involve Stakeholders Early:**

    Involving stakeholders early in the decision-making process helps ensure that their perspectives are considered and that they feel a sense of ownership over the outcome.

    - **Gather Input:** Before making significant decisions, gather input from the board, residents, and other relevant parties.

This could be through surveys, focus groups, or open forums. Understanding the needs and preferences of the community helps inform better decisions.

- **Transparency:** Be transparent about the decision-making process, including the criteria used to evaluate options and the timeline for making a decision. This transparency builds trust and reduces the likelihood of disputes.

- **Encourage Participation:** Encourage participation by making it easy for stakeholders to contribute their ideas and opinions. For example, hold community meetings at convenient times, provide online surveys, or create opportunities for informal discussions.

2. **Facilitate Productive Meetings:**

   Meetings are a common forum for decision-making in community associations. To ensure that meetings are productive and collaborative, consider the following strategies:

   - **Structured Agendas:** Prepare a structured agenda that outlines the topics to be discussed, the time allocated for each, and the desired outcomes. Share the agenda with participants in advance so they can prepare.

   - **Focus on Solutions:** Keep discussions focused on finding solutions rather than dwelling on problems. Encourage participants to propose actionable ideas and work toward consensus.

   - **Respectful Dialogue:** Foster an environment of respectful dialogue, where everyone's opinions are valued and heard. Set ground rules for the meeting to ensure that discussions remain constructive and on-topic.

3. Use Data to Inform Decisions:

Data-driven decision-making is a powerful tool in community management. By using data to inform decisions, you can make more objective, informed choices that are in the best interest of the community.

- **Financial Data:** Use financial reports, budget forecasts, and reserve studies to guide decisions related to spending, assessments, and capital improvements. Financial data provides a clear picture of the community's resources and helps prioritize projects.

- **Survey Results:** Leverage survey results and feedback from residents to make decisions that reflect the community's preferences. This data can be especially useful when considering changes to amenities, rules, or services.

- **Maintenance Records:** Maintenance records and inspection reports can inform decisions about repairs, upgrades, and vendor contracts. Understanding the condition of the property helps prioritize maintenance projects and allocate resources effectively.

4. Build Consensus:

Building consensus among stakeholders is crucial for making decisions that are widely supported and accepted. Here's how to foster consensus-building:

- **Inclusive Discussions:** Ensure that all voices are heard during discussions, including those of board members, residents, and other stakeholders. Inclusive discussions lead to more well-rounded decisions.

- **Compromise:** Be willing to compromise when necessary. Finding a middle ground that satisfies most stakeholders is often more beneficial than a decision that is polarizing or divisive.

- **Communicate the Decision:** Once a decision has been made, communicate it clearly to all stakeholders. Explain the reasoning behind the decision, how it was reached, and what the next steps are. Clear communication helps manage expectations and ensures that everyone is on the same page.

5. **Implementing Decisions Effectively:**

After a decision is made, it's important to implement it effectively to achieve the desired outcomes. Here's how to ensure successful implementation:

- **Action Plans:** Develop a detailed action plan that outlines the steps needed to implement the decision, the timeline, and the responsible parties. This plan serves as a roadmap for execution.

- **Monitor Progress:** Regularly monitor progress toward implementation, and provide updates to the board and residents as needed. If challenges arise, address them promptly and adjust the plan as necessary.

- **Evaluate Outcomes:** After implementation, evaluate the outcomes to determine if the decision achieved the desired results. Solicit feedback from stakeholders to understand the impact and identify areas for improvement.

CONCLUSION

Building strong partnerships with the board of directors and the community is essential for successful community association management. By fostering effective communication, understanding board dynamics, engaging with residents, and collaborating on decision-making, you can create a harmonious and thriving community.

Throughout this chapter, we've explored strategies for building these partnerships, including practical examples and actionable advice. Whether you're new to the industry or looking to enhance your management skills, these strategies will help you navigate the complexities of community management and achieve positive outcomes for the communities you serve.

Remember, the key to successful community management lies in your ability to build trust, foster collaboration, and create a sense of community. By applying the principles discussed in this chapter, you'll be well-equipped to build strong, lasting partnerships that benefit both the board and the residents, leading to a more harmonious and well-managed community.

CHAPTER 4

DECODING PROFESSIONAL CREDENTIALS

Professional credentials are a significant asset in the world of community association management. They serve as a testament to a manager's expertise, dedication, and commitment to maintaining high standards in their field. For someone new to the community association industry, understanding these credentials can be crucial to shaping a successful career. Credentials not only enhance your knowledge and skills but also position you as a trusted professional in the eyes of boards, residents, and employers.

This chapter will guide you through the various certifications and designations available to community association managers. We'll explore what each credential entails, the benefits of obtaining them, and how they can impact your career. Additionally, personal stories and experiences from seasoned professionals will highlight the importance of continuous learning and professional growth.

THE IMPORTANCE OF PROFESSIONAL CREDENTIALS

Before diving into specific certifications, it's essential to understand why professional credentials matter in community association management.

1. **Demonstrating Expertise:**

    Credentials provide a formal recognition of your knowledge and skills in community management. They show that you have met industry standards and are equipped to handle the complexities of managing residential communities. This expertise is critical when dealing with boards of directors, residents, and service providers, as it builds trust and credibility.

2. **Career Advancement:**

Holding certifications can open doors to higher-level positions and increased responsibilities. Many employers prefer or even require certain credentials for managerial roles. Additionally, having these certifications can distinguish you from other candidates in a competitive job market, giving you an edge when applying for new positions or seeking promotions.

3. **Commitment to Professionalism:**

Pursuing certifications demonstrates your commitment to professionalism and continuous improvement. It shows that you are dedicated to staying updated with the latest industry trends, best practices, and regulatory changes. This commitment can lead to greater respect and recognition within the industry and among your peers.

4. **Enhancing Service Quality:**

The knowledge gained through certification programs enables you to provide higher quality service to the communities you manage. Whether it's through improved financial management, better communication strategies, or more effective governance, your enhanced skills contribute to the overall success of the communities under your care.

5. **Networking Opportunities:**

Many certification programs offer opportunities to connect with other professionals in the industry. Whether through conferences, online forums, or local chapters, networking with peers can lead to valuable insights, job opportunities, and professional support.

KEY CERTIFICATIONS AND DESIGNATIONS

Several organizations offer certifications and designations tailored to community association management. Below, we explore some of the most recognized credentials in the industry:

1. **Certified Manager of Community Associations (CMCA)**

   Offered by: Community Associations Institute (CAI)

   Overview: The CMCA is often the first step for many community managers pursuing professional credentials. It is a foundational certification that covers the essential aspects of community association management, including governance, legal compliance, financial management, facilities management, and risk management.

   Requirements:

   - **Education:** Candidates must complete a prerequisite course, such as the M-100: Essentials of Community Association Management, offered by CAI. This course provides a comprehensive introduction to community management and prepares candidates for the CMCA exam.

   - **Exam:** After completing the prerequisite course, candidates must pass the CMCA exam, which tests their knowledge of community association management principles.

   Benefits:

   - **Professional Recognition:** Earning the CMCA credential establishes you as a qualified and capable manager in the field.

   - **Foundation for Further Certifications:** The CMCA serves as a stepping stone for more advanced certifications, such as the AMS and PCAM.

   - **Career Opportunities:** Many employers consider the CMCA a minimum requirement for management positions, making it an essential credential for career advancement.

Personal Story: *"When I first entered the community association management industry, I felt overwhelmed by the breadth of responsibilities. Pursuing the CMCA credential helped me gain a solid understanding of the fundamentals and gave me the confidence to manage my first community. The knowledge I gained through the M-100 course and the CMCA exam was invaluable, and it set the stage for my continued professional development."* — Sarah, CMCA, AMS

2. **Association Management Specialist (AMS)**

Offered by: Community Associations Institute (CAI)

Overview: The AMS designation is designed for experienced managers who have already obtained the CMCA and are looking to deepen their expertise. This designation focuses on advanced management practices, professional ethics, and leadership in the community association industry.

Requirements:

- **CMCA Certification:** Candidates must already hold the CMCA certification.
- **Experience:** A minimum of two years of experience in community association management is required.
- **Advanced Coursework:** Candidates must complete two additional CAI courses, such as M-201: Facilities Management or M-203: Community Leadership. These courses delve into specialized areas of community management.
- **Ethics:** Candidates must adhere to CAI's Professional Manager Code of Ethics.

Benefits:

- **Advanced Knowledge:** The AMS designation provides in-depth knowledge in areas critical to successful community management, such as risk management, maintenance planning, and leadership.
- **Increased Earning Potential:** Managers with the AMS designation often command higher salaries due to their advanced skills and experience.
- **Pathway to PCAM:** The AMS is a prerequisite for the prestigious PCAM designation, making it an essential step for those seeking to reach the highest levels of the profession.

Personal Story: *"After earning my CMCA, I knew I wanted to continue advancing in my career. The AMS designation challenged me to expand my knowledge and think more strategically about the communities I manage. The advanced courses were rigorous, but they provided me with the tools I needed to tackle complex issues and lead with confidence. Achieving the AMS was a turning point in my career."* — David, CMCA, AMS, PCAM

3. **Professional Community Association Manager (PCAM)**

   Offered by: Community Associations Institute (CAI)

   Overview: The PCAM designation is the pinnacle of professional credentials in community association management. It is designed for the most experienced managers who have demonstrated exceptional leadership, knowledge, and dedication to the industry.

Requirements:

CMCA and AMS Certifications: Candidates must hold both the CMCA and AMS certifications.

- **Experience:** A minimum of five years of experience in community association management is required.
- **Advanced Coursework:** Candidates must complete a series of advanced CAI courses, including M-300: Ethics, Rules, and Conduct, and M-350: Manager and the Law.
- **Case Study:** Candidates must complete an intensive case study of a community association. This capstone project requires candidates to analyze the community's operations, governance, and financial management, and present recommendations for improvement.
- **PCAM Review Panel:** Candidates must successfully present their case study to a panel of PCAM designees for evaluation.

Benefits:

- **Prestige and Recognition:** The PCAM designation is highly respected in the industry and signifies the highest level of professional achievement.
- **Leadership Opportunities:** PCAM designees are often sought after for leadership roles, such as executive director or regional manager positions, due to their extensive experience and expertise.
- **Networking:** As a PCAM, you join an elite group of professionals, providing access to valuable networking opportunities and industry connections.

Personal Story: *"Achieving the PCAM designation was the culmination of years of hard work and dedication. The case study project was incredibly challenging, but it pushed me to apply everything I had learned throughout my career. Presenting my findings to the review panel was nerve-wracking, but the feedback I received was invaluable.*

Earning the PCAM has opened doors to new opportunities and solidified my reputation as a leader in the industry." — Linda, CMCA, AMS, PCAM

4. **Accredited Residential Manager (ARM)**

   Offered by: Institute of Real Estate Management (IREM)

   Overview: The ARM certification is designed for managers of residential properties, including community associations, apartment buildings, and other residential real estate. This certification focuses on property management principles, financial management, marketing, and maintenance.

   Requirements:

   - **Experience:** Candidates must have at least one year of experience in residential property management.
   - **Coursework:** Candidates must complete the ARM course, which covers topics such as leasing, marketing, financial operations, and maintenance management.
   - **Exam:** Candidates must pass the ARM certification exam, which tests their knowledge of residential property management.
   - **Ethics:** Candidates must adhere to IREM's Code of Professional Ethics.

   Benefits:

   - **Specialized Knowledge:** The ARM certification provides specialized knowledge in managing residential properties, making it particularly valuable for community managers who oversee multi-unit buildings or apartment complexes.
   - **Industry Recognition:** The ARM designation is recognized by employers and peers as a mark of excellence in residential property management.

- **Pathway to CPM:** The ARM certification is a stepping stone to the Certified Property Manager (CPM) designation, which is one of the most prestigious credentials in real estate management.

Personal Story: *"When I transitioned from managing single-family homes to overseeing a large condominium complex, I realized I needed to enhance my skills in residential property management. The ARM certification provided me with the knowledge I needed to effectively manage the property, from leasing to maintenance. It was a game-changer for my career, and it set me on the path to eventually earning my CPM."* — John, ARM, CPM

5. **Certified Property Manager (CPM)**

   Offered by: Institute of Real Estate Management (IREM)

   Overview: The CPM designation is one of the most respected credentials in real estate and property management. It is designed for experienced managers who oversee a diverse portfolio of properties, including community associations, commercial properties, and residential buildings.

   Requirements:

   - **ARM or Equivalent Experience:** Candidates must have earned the ARM certification or have equivalent experience in property management.
   - **Advanced Coursework:** Candidates must complete a series of advanced courses, covering topics such as asset management, financial analysis, human resources, and legal compliance.
   - **Experience:** Candidates must have at least three years of experience managing real estate assets.

- **Management Plan:** Candidates must submit a detailed management plan for a property, demonstrating their ability to analyze, plan, and execute management strategies.
- **Exam:** Candidates must pass the CPM certification exam, which tests their comprehensive knowledge of property management.
- **Ethics:** Candidates must adhere to IREM's Code of Professional Ethics.

Benefits:

- **Comprehensive Expertise:** The CPM designation signifies a high level of expertise in all aspects of property management, from financial planning to asset management.
- **Leadership Roles:** CPM designees are often considered for senior management and executive roles due to their extensive experience and advanced skills.
- **Global Recognition:** The CPM designation is recognized internationally, providing opportunities for career advancement both within the U.S. and abroad.

Personal Story: *"Earning the CPM designation was a pivotal moment in my career. The advanced coursework challenged me to think strategically about property management, and the management plan project allowed me to showcase my skills to potential employers. Since earning my CPM, I've taken on more complex properties and moved into a regional management role. The designation has truly elevated my career."* — Emily, CPM

3. **Certified Apartment Manager (CAM)**

   Offered by: National Apartment Association (NAA)

   Overview: The CAM certification is specifically designed for managers of apartment communities. This credential focuses on the unique challenges of managing multi-family housing, including leasing, marketing, resident retention, and maintenance.

Requirements:

- **Experience:** Candidates must have at least 12 months of experience in apartment management.
- **Coursework:** Candidates must complete the CAM course, which covers topics such as marketing, financial management, legal compliance, and resident relations.
- **Exam:** Candidates must pass the CAM certification exam, which tests their knowledge of apartment management.
- **Continuing Education:** Candidates must complete continuing education courses to maintain their certification.

Benefits:

- **Industry-Specific Knowledge:** The CAM certification provides targeted knowledge for managing apartment communities, making it ideal for managers in the multi-family housing sector.
- **Improved Resident Satisfaction:** The skills gained through the CAM program can help managers improve resident satisfaction, retention rates, and overall community success.
- **Career Growth:** The CAM designation can lead to career advancement opportunities, such as moving from a property-level management role to a regional management position.

Personal Story: *"Managing an apartment community is different from other types of residential properties, and I wanted to ensure I had the skills to succeed. The CAM certification provided me with the tools I needed to effectively manage leasing, marketing, and resident relations. Since earning my CAM, I've been able to increase resident retention and improve the overall performance of the community."* — Jessica, CAM

7. **Project Management Professional (PMP)**

    Offered by: Project Management Institute (PMI)

    Overview: The PMP certification is a globally recognized credential in project management. While not specific to community association management, it is highly valuable for managers who oversee large-scale projects, such as capital improvements, renovations, or new developments.

    Requirements:
    - **Experience:** Candidates must have a minimum of three years of project management experience, including leading and directing projects.
    - **Education:** Candidates must complete 35 hours of project management education, such as a PMP prep course.
    - **Exam:** Candidates must pass the PMP certification exam, which tests their knowledge of project management processes, methodologies, and best practices.

    Benefits:
    - **Project Management Expertise:** The PMP certification equips managers with advanced project management skills, making them more effective in planning, executing, and closing projects.
    - **Versatility:** The PMP is a versatile credential that is applicable across various industries, including community association management, real estate, construction, and more.
    - **Higher Salaries:** PMP-certified professionals often command higher salaries due to their specialized skills in managing complex projects.

    Personal Story: *"As a community manager, I frequently oversee large renovation projects and capital improvements. The PMP certification has been instrumental in helping me manage these projects more* *effectively, from initial planning to final execution. The skills I gained through the PMP program have not only improved my project management abilities but also enhanced my overall management approach." —* Michael, PMP

CHOOSING THE RIGHT CREDENTIALS FOR YOUR CAREER

With so many certifications and designations available, it can be challenging to decide which ones are the best fit for your career goals. Here are some factors to consider when choosing the right credentials:

1. **Assess Your Career Goals:**
   - **Entry-Level Managers:** If you're just starting in community association management, the CMCA or CAM certifications are excellent starting points. They provide foundational knowledge and set the stage for further advancement.
   - **Mid-Level Managers:** If you have a few years of experience and are looking to take on more responsibility, consider pursuing the AMS, ARM, or PMP certifications. These credentials will deepen your expertise and prepare you for more complex roles.
   - **Senior Managers:** For those with significant experience, the PCAM or CPM designations are ideal for advancing to executive roles or managing larger portfolios.

2. **Evaluate Your Current Skills and Experience:**
   - **Industry-Specific Knowledge:** If you're focused on a particular area of community management, such as apartment communities or residential properties, choose a certification that aligns with your expertise, such as the CAM or ARM.
   - **Project Management:** If you frequently manage large projects, the PMP certification can provide valuable skills that are applicable across various types of projects.

3. **Consider Your Employer's Requirements:**
   - **Job Requirements:** Some employers may require specific certifications for certain positions. Review job descriptions and speak with your employer to understand which credentials are most valued within your organization.
   - **Career Advancement:** If you're aiming for a promotion, find out which certifications are required or preferred for the role you're targeting. This information can help you prioritize your certification goals.

4. **Plan for Continuing Education:**
   - **Ongoing Learning:** Many certifications require continuing education to maintain the credential. Consider how you will meet these requirements and whether the certification aligns with your commitment to lifelong learning.
   - **Professional Development:** Look for certifications that offer opportunities for professional development, such as conferences, workshops, and networking events. These opportunities can help you stay current with industry trends and expand your professional network.

5. **Seek Advice from Mentors and Peers:**
   - **Mentorship:** Reach out to mentors or colleagues who have obtained the certifications you're considering. Their insights and experiences can help you make an informed decision.
   - **Networking:** Attend industry events or join professional associations to connect with other community managers. Networking can provide valuable advice on which certifications are most respected and beneficial in the industry.

THE PATH FORWARD: COMMITMENT TO PROFESSIONAL EXCELLENCE

Earning professional credentials is a significant investment in your career, but it's only the beginning of your journey toward professional excellence. Here's how to continue growing and thriving in the community association management industry:

1. **Set Clear Goals:**
   - **Short-Term Goals:** Identify short-term goals, such as obtaining your first certification or completing a specific course. Setting achievable milestones helps you stay motivated and focused on your career development.
   - **Long-Term Goals:** Consider where you want to be in five or ten years. Whether it's achieving the PCAM designation or moving into a leadership role, having a long-term vision will guide your professional growth.

2. **Embrace Continuous Learning:**
   - **Stay Informed:** The community association industry is constantly evolving, with new regulations, technologies, and best practices emerging regularly. Stay informed by reading industry publications, attending webinars, and participating in continuing education courses.
   - **Pursue Advanced Certifications:** As you gain experience, continue pursuing advanced certifications that align with your career goals. Each new credential you earn will build on your existing knowledge and open up new opportunities.

3. **Share Your Knowledge:**
   - **Mentorship:** Consider becoming a mentor to newer community managers. Sharing your knowledge and experiences not only helps others but also reinforces your own understanding of the industry.

- **Teaching and Speaking:** Look for opportunities to teach courses, lead workshops, or speak at industry conferences. These activities enhance your credibility and position you as a thought leader in the field.

4. **Network and Collaborate:**
   - **Join Professional Associations:** Becoming an active member of professional associations, such as CAI or IREM, provides access to valuable resources, networking opportunities, and industry events.
   - **Collaborate with Peers:** Collaborate with other community managers to share best practices, solve challenges, and develop innovative solutions. Building a strong professional network is essential for long-term success.

5. **Maintain Ethical Standards:**
   - **Adhere to Codes of Ethics:** All professional certifications come with a code of ethics that you must adhere to. Maintaining high ethical standards is crucial for building trust and credibility with boards, residents, and colleagues.
   - **Lead by Example:** As a credentialed professional, you are a role model for others in the industry. Lead by example by demonstrating integrity, professionalism, and a commitment to excellence in all aspects of your work.

CONCLUSION

Decoding professional credentials in community association management is an essential step toward building a successful and fulfilling career. Whether you're just starting or are an experienced manager looking to advance, the certifications and designations discussed in this chapter offer a clear path to professional growth and development.

By understanding the requirements, benefits, and career implications of each credential, you can make informed decisions that align with your goals and aspirations. Remember, pursuing these credentials is not just about gaining a title; it's about continuously improving your skills, expanding your knowledge, and becoming a more effective and respected leader in the community association industry.

As you move forward on your professional journey, keep in mind the importance of continuous learning, networking, and ethical practice. The dedication you invest in earning and maintaining your credentials will not only benefit your career but also contribute to the success and well-being of the communities you manage.

CHAPTER 5

MASTERING COMMUNICATION IN COMMUNITY MANAGEMENT

Effective communication is one of the most critical skills a community manager can possess. It serves as the foundation for building strong relationships with residents, board members, vendors, and contractors. Whether you're addressing a resident's concern, facilitating a board meeting, or negotiating with a vendor, the way you communicate can significantly impact the success of your management efforts. For someone new to the community association industry, mastering communication is essential for navigating the complex dynamics of residential communities and ensuring smooth operations.

In this chapter, we'll explore the various aspects of communication in community management, including the importance of clarity and consistency, the use of different communication channels, and techniques for active listening. We'll also delve into strategies for handling difficult conversations and how to leverage technology to enhance communication within the community. By the end of this chapter, you'll have a comprehensive understanding of how to communicate effectively with all stakeholders, fostering a culture of transparency, trust, and engagement.

THE IMPORTANCE OF CLEAR AND CONSISTENT COMMUNICATION

Clear and consistent communication is the bedrock of effective community management. When communication is clear, it minimizes misunderstandings, reduces conflicts, and ensures that all stakeholders are well-informed. Consistency in communication helps to build trust and credibility, as it shows that you are reliable and that information is shared in a timely and accurate manner.

1. **Clarity in Communication:**

    Clarity means ensuring that your message is understood by the recipient exactly as you intend. This involves using plain language, avoiding jargon, and being precise in your instructions or information. Clarity is especially important when communicating rules, policies, or decisions that affect the community.

    - **Use Simple Language:** Avoid using technical terms or industry jargon that residents or board members may not understand. Instead, use simple, straightforward language to convey your message.

    - **Be Specific:** Provide detailed information to avoid ambiguity. For example, if you're informing residents about a maintenance schedule, specify the dates, times, and areas affected rather than giving vague details.

    - **Repeat Key Points:** When communicating important information, such as changes in community rules or upcoming events, repeat key points to reinforce understanding. You can do this by summarizing the main points at the end of your message or using bullet points for emphasis.

2. **Consistency in Communication:**

    Consistency in communication ensures that information is conveyed in a uniform manner across all channels and interactions. This helps prevent confusion and ensures that all stakeholders receive the same message, regardless of how or when they receive it.

- **Standardize Messaging:** Use templates for common communications, such as newsletters, meeting notices, or policy updates. This ensures that your messaging is consistent in tone, style, and content.

- **Regular Updates:** Provide regular updates to residents and board members to keep them informed about community operations, projects, and events. Consistent communication helps build trust and keeps everyone on the same page.

- **Align Communication Channels:** Ensure that the same information is communicated across all channels, whether it's through email, the community website, or social media. This prevents discrepancies and ensures that everyone has access to the same information.

CASE STUDY: THE IMPACT OF CLEAR AND CONSISTENT COMMUNICATION

Consider a community manager named Lisa, who manages a mid-sized homeowners association. When she first started in her role, she noticed that residents often complained about not being informed about important events, leading to frustration and low participation.

To address this, Lisa implemented the following communication strategies:

- **Monthly Newsletters:** She introduced a monthly newsletter that provided updates on community projects, upcoming events, and board decisions. The newsletter was distributed via email and posted on the community's website.

- **Standardized Templates:** Lisa created standardized templates for common communications, such as maintenance notices and policy updates. This ensured that all messages were consistent and clear.
- **Resident Surveys:** To gather feedback and ensure that residents were satisfied with the communication, Lisa conducted regular surveys. She used the feedback to improve the clarity and frequency of her updates.

As a result of these efforts, resident complaints decreased, and participation in community events increased. Lisa's clear and consistent communication helped build trust with residents and improved overall satisfaction within the community.

EXPLORING DIFFERENT COMMUNICATION CHANNELS

In community management, effective communication requires using a variety of channels to reach all stakeholders. Different channels serve different purposes, and understanding how to use each one effectively is key to ensuring that your message is received and understood by everyone.

1. **Traditional Communication Channels:**

   Traditional communication channels include methods such as face-to-face meetings, printed newsletters, bulletin boards, and phone calls. While these channels may seem outdated to some, they remain valuable tools for reaching certain segments of the community, particularly older residents or those who prefer more personal interactions.

   - **Face-to-Face Meetings:** In-person meetings, whether with residents, board members, or vendors, provide an opportunity for direct interaction and immediate feedback. These meetings are particularly useful for discussing complex issues, resolving conflicts, or building rapport.

- **Printed Newsletters:** Printed newsletters are an effective way to communicate with residents who may not have access to digital platforms. They can be distributed through mailboxes or at community events and are especially useful for sharing updates, reminders, and important announcements.

- **Bulletin Boards:** Community bulletin boards, located in common areas such as clubhouses or lobbies, serve as a central point for posting notices, event flyers, and other important information. They are a convenient way to keep residents informed of ongoing activities.

- **Phone Calls:** While email and messaging apps are common today, phone calls remain an important tool for more personal or urgent communication. A quick phone call can resolve misunderstandings, answer questions, or provide reassurance to residents who prefer verbal communication.

2. **Digital Communication Channels:**

Digital communication channels have become increasingly popular due to their convenience, speed, and ability to reach a large audience quickly. These channels include email, community websites, social media, and messaging apps.

- **Email:** Email is one of the most widely used communication tools in community management. It allows you to send updates, notices, and important information directly to residents and board members. Email is particularly useful for distributing newsletters, meeting minutes, and policy changes.

- **Community Websites:** A dedicated community website serves as a central hub for all information related to the community. It can include sections for news updates, event calendars, governing documents, and contact information. Websites provide residents with easy access to information at any time.

- **Social Media:** Social media platforms like Facebook, Twitter, and Nextdoor offer a way to engage with residents in a more informal and interactive manner. These platforms are ideal for sharing community news, promoting events, and encouraging resident participation.

- **Messaging Apps:** Messaging apps like WhatsApp, Slack, or even text messaging can facilitate real-time communication among residents, board members, and management. They are particularly useful for urgent notifications or quick updates, such as maintenance alerts or security issues.

3. **Hybrid Communication Strategies:**

To ensure that all residents are reached, consider using a hybrid communication strategy that combines traditional and digital channels. This approach ensures that information is accessible to everyone, regardless of their preferred communication method.

- **Integrated Communication Plan:** Develop an integrated communication plan that outlines how different channels will be used for various types of communication. For example, major announcements could be communicated through email, social media, and bulletin boards simultaneously.

- **Resident Preferences:** Survey residents to understand their preferred communication channels. Use this information to tailor your communication strategy, ensuring that residents receive information in the format they prefer.

- **Cross-Promote Channels:** Encourage residents to engage with multiple communication channels by cross-promoting them. For example, you can include a reminder in the printed newsletter to visit the community website for more detailed information or to follow the community's social media page.

CASE STUDY: EFFECTIVE USE OF HYBRID COMMUNICATION CHANNELS

Mark, a community manager for a large condominium association, noticed that while some residents were highly engaged on the community's social media page, others preferred traditional methods like bulletin boards and printed newsletters. To bridge the gap, Mark implemented a hybrid communication strategy:

- **Integrated Announcements:** Mark ensured that all major announcements, such as policy changes or upcoming events, were communicated through multiple channels: email, the community website, social media, and printed flyers posted on bulletin boards.

- **Customized Updates:** Based on resident preferences, Mark sent customized updates through different channels. For example, residents who preferred digital communication received updates via email and social media, while those who preferred traditional methods received printed newsletters.

- **Engagement Analytics:** Mark tracked engagement across different channels to see which were most effective. He used this data to refine the communication strategy, ensuring that residents remained informed and engaged.

The hybrid approach led to increased resident satisfaction, as everyone felt included and informed regardless of their preferred communication method.

TECHNIQUES FOR ACTIVE LISTENING

Active listening is a critical skill for community managers, as it allows you to fully understand the concerns, needs, and feedback of residents, board members, and other stakeholders. Active listening goes beyond simply hearing what someone is saying; it involves engaging with the speaker, showing empathy, and responding thoughtfully.

1. **The Principles of Active Listening:**

    Active listening involves several key principles that help ensure effective communication:

    -   **Full Attention:** Give the speaker your undivided attention. This means putting away distractions, maintaining eye contact (in face-to-face interactions), and focusing on what the speaker is saying.

    -   **Reflecting and Paraphrasing:** Reflecting involves summarizing what the speaker has said in your own words. This shows that you are listening and allows you to confirm your understanding. For example, you might say, "It sounds like you're concerned about the new parking policy because it might affect guest parking. Is that correct?"

    -   **Empathy:** Show empathy by acknowledging the speaker's feelings and concerns. Even if you don't agree with their perspective, it's important to validate their emotions. For example, "I understand that the recent maintenance issues have been frustrating for you. Let's see how we can address this."

    -   **Asking Questions:** Ask open-ended questions to encourage the speaker to elaborate on their thoughts. This helps you gather more information and shows that you are interested in their viewpoint. For example, "Can you tell me more about what happened during the recent board meeting?"

- **Avoiding Interruptions:** Allow the speaker to express their thoughts without interruption. Interrupting can make the speaker feel unheard and can disrupt the flow of communication.

2. **Applying Active Listening in Community Management:** Active listening is particularly important in situations where residents or board members have concerns or complaints. Here's how to apply active listening in different scenarios:

   - **Handling Complaints:** When a resident comes to you with a complaint, listen actively to understand the root of the issue. Reflect their concerns back to them, show empathy, and ask clarifying questions if needed. This approach helps de-escalate the situation and demonstrates that you are taking their concerns seriously.

   - **Board Meetings:** During board meetings, use active listening to ensure that all members feel heard and that their input is considered. Reflect and paraphrase key points to confirm your understanding, and encourage open dialogue by asking questions.

   - **Vendor Negotiations:** When negotiating with vendors, active listening helps you understand their needs and constraints. This can lead to more collaborative discussions and better outcomes for both parties.

CASE STUDY: THE POWER OF ACTIVE LISTENING

Jane, a community manager for a gated community, encountered a situation where a group of residents was upset about a new landscaping project. The residents felt that the project was unnecessary and that the funds could be better spent elsewhere.

Instead of dismissing their concerns, Jane applied active listening techniques:

- **Full Attention:** Jane invited the residents to meet with her and gave them her full attention during the meeting. She put aside her phone and notes to focus solely on the conversation.
- **Reflecting and Paraphrasing:** As the residents expressed their concerns, Jane reflected their points back to them. For example, she said, "It seems like you're worried that the landscaping project isn't a priority right now and that the funds could be used for other improvements. Is that correct?"
- **Empathy:** Jane acknowledged the residents' concerns by saying, "I understand that you're concerned about how the community's funds are being used. It's important that we prioritize projects that benefit everyone."
- **Asking Questions:** Jane asked open-ended questions to gather more information, such as, "What other projects do you think should be prioritized?" and "How do you feel the landscaping project might impact the community?"

Through active listening, Jane was able to address the residents' concerns and explain the rationale behind the landscaping project. She also took their feedback to the board, which led to a decision to re-evaluate the project's timing and scope. The residents appreciated Jane's willingness to listen and involve them in the decision-making process, leading to a more positive relationship with the community.

HANDLING DIFFICULT CONVERSATIONS WITH TACT

Difficult conversations are an inevitable part of community management, whether you're addressing a resident's complaint, delivering unwelcome news, or resolving conflicts between stakeholders.

Handling these conversations with tact requires preparation, empathy, and clear communication.

1. **Preparing for Difficult Conversations:**

    Preparation is key to handling difficult conversations effectively. Before initiating a difficult conversation, take the following steps:

    - **Gather Information:** Collect all relevant information about the issue at hand. This might include reviewing past communications, gathering data, or consulting with other stakeholders. Having a complete understanding of the situation will help you address concerns more effectively.

    - **Plan Your Approach:** Think about how you will present the information and what you want to achieve from the conversation. Consider the potential reactions of the other party and how you will respond. Planning your approach helps you stay focused and calm during the conversation.

    - **Choose the Right Setting:** Select a setting that is private and conducive to a productive discussion. Avoid public places where the conversation could be overheard or where the other party might feel uncomfortable.

2. **Conducting the Conversation:**

    During the conversation, focus on maintaining a respectful and constructive tone. Here are some strategies to help you navigate difficult discussions:

    - **Start with Empathy:** Begin the conversation by acknowledging the other party's feelings or concerns. This helps to build rapport and shows that you are approaching the conversation with empathy. For example, "I understand that this situation has been challenging for you, and I want to work together to find a solution."

- **Be Honest and Direct:** While it's important to be empathetic, it's also crucial to be honest and direct about the issue at hand. Avoid sugar-coating the situation or being vague. Clearly state the facts and explain the reasoning behind your decisions or actions.

- **Focus on Solutions:** Rather than dwelling on the problem, steer the conversation toward finding a resolution. Ask for the other party's input and work together to identify potential solutions. This collaborative approach helps to defuse tension and encourages a positive outcome.

- **Stay Calm:** In difficult conversations, emotions can run high. It's important to remain calm and composed, even if the other party becomes upset or confrontational. If the conversation becomes too heated, suggest taking a short break to allow both parties to regain composure.

3. **Following Up After the Conversation:**

    After the conversation, it's important to follow up to ensure that the issue has been resolved and that both parties are satisfied with the outcome.

    - **Summarize the Discussion:** Send a follow-up email summarizing the key points of the conversation and any agreed-upon actions. This provides a written record of the discussion and ensures that both parties are on the same page.

    - **Monitor Progress:** If the conversation resulted in a plan of action, monitor progress to ensure that it is being implemented. Check in with the other party periodically to see how things are going and if any further assistance is needed.

    - **Reflect on the Experience:** Take some time to reflect on the conversation and consider what went well and what could have been improved. Use this reflection to refine your approach to handling difficult conversations in the future.

CASE STUDY: NAVIGATING A DIFFICULT CONVERSATION

Paul, a community manager for a large homeowners association, needed to address a sensitive issue with a resident who had repeatedly violated the community's noise policy. Other residents had complained, and the situation was creating tension in the community.

Paul approached the conversation with the following steps:

- **Preparation:** Paul reviewed the community's noise policy and the specific complaints that had been filed. He also considered the resident's possible reactions and planned how he would address them.

- **Starting with Empathy:** Paul began the conversation by acknowledging the resident's perspective: "I understand that you enjoy hosting gatherings, and I want to find a way to ensure that you can do so while also respecting the peace and quiet that your neighbors value."

- **Being Direct:** Paul then explained the issue clearly and directly: "There have been several complaints about noise levels during your gatherings, which exceed the limits set by our community's noise policy. It's important that we address this to maintain a positive living environment for everyone."

- **Focusing on Solutions:** Paul worked with the resident to identify potential solutions, such as moving gatherings indoors after a certain time or using quieter entertainment options. They agreed on a plan that respected both the resident's social activities and the community's noise policy.

- **Follow-Up:** After the conversation, Paul sent a follow-up email summarizing the discussion and the agreed-upon actions. He also checked in with the resident a few weeks later to see how things were going and to offer further support if needed.

By handling the conversation with tact and focusing on solutions, Paul was able to resolve the issue without creating further tension. The resident appreciated Paul's respectful approach, and the noise complaints subsequently decreased.

LEVERAGING TECHNOLOGY TO ENHANCE COMMUNICATION

In today's digital age, technology plays a crucial role in enhancing communication within community management. Leveraging the right tools can improve efficiency, foster engagement, and ensure that information is shared effectively with all stakeholders.

1. **Communication Platforms:**

    There are several communication platforms that can streamline interactions between community managers, residents, and board members. These platforms offer various features, such as messaging, document sharing, and event scheduling.

    - **Community Management Software:** Dedicated community management software platforms, such as TownSq, Buildium, or AppFolio, offer integrated communication tools that allow you to send announcements, share documents, and manage resident requests all in one place. These platforms help centralize communication and make it easier to keep track of interactions.

    - **Email Marketing Tools:** Tools like Mailchimp or Constant Contact can be used to send newsletters, updates, and announcements to residents. These platforms allow you to segment your audience, track open rates, and ensure that your messages reach the right people.

- **Social Media Management:** Social media management tools like Hootsuite or Buffer help you manage multiple social media accounts, schedule posts, and engage with residents online. These tools are particularly useful for promoting community events and sharing news in real time.

2. **Enhancing Engagement Through Technology:**

   Technology can also be used to enhance resident engagement by making it easier for them to participate in community activities, provide feedback, and stay informed.

   - **Online Surveys:** Use online survey tools like SurveyMonkey or Google Forms to gather feedback from residents on various topics, such as community rules, amenities, or events. Surveys are a great way to involve residents in decision-making and ensure that their voices are heard.

   - **Virtual Meetings:** Virtual meeting platforms like Zoom or Microsoft Teams allow you to hold board meetings, town halls, or committee meetings remotely. Virtual meetings make it easier for residents to attend and participate, especially if they have busy schedules or live far from the community.

   - **Event Management:** Use event management tools like Eventbrite or Meetup to organize and promote community events. These platforms allow residents to RSVP, receive event reminders, and share the event with others.

3. **Promoting Transparency Through Technology:**

   Transparency is key to building trust within the community. Technology can help promote transparency by making important information easily accessible to residents.

   - **Document Sharing:** Use cloud storage platforms like Google Drive or Dropbox to share important documents with residents, such as meeting minutes, financial reports, or governing documents. These platforms allow residents to access information at any time and from any device.

- **Real-Time Updates:** Use community management software or social media to provide real-time updates on maintenance schedules, project progress, or emergency alerts. Keeping residents informed in real time helps build trust and ensures that they are always aware of what's happening in the community.

CASE STUDY: LEVERAGING TECHNOLOGY FOR BETTER COMMUNICATION

Samantha, a community manager for a large condominium complex, recognized that residents were often frustrated by a lack of timely communication about maintenance issues and upcoming events. To address this, she decided to leverage technology to enhance communication within the community.

- **Community Management Software:** Samantha implemented a community management software platform that allowed residents to submit maintenance requests, view community documents, and receive announcements. The platform also included a messaging feature that enabled Samantha to communicate directly with residents.
- **Email Marketing:** Samantha used an email marketing tool to send out weekly newsletters that included updates on maintenance schedules, upcoming events, and board decisions. The tool allowed her to segment the email list based on resident preferences, ensuring that everyone received relevant information.
- **Online Surveys:** To gather feedback on the new communication initiatives, Samantha used an online survey tool. The

survey results showed that residents were highly satisfied with the improved communication and appreciated the transparency.

- **Virtual Meetings:** Samantha also began hosting virtual town hall meetings to discuss important community issues and gather resident input. The virtual format made it easier for residents to attend and participate, leading to more engagement.

By leveraging technology, Samantha was able to improve communication within the community, increase resident satisfaction, and foster a more engaged and informed community.

FOSTERING A CULTURE OF TRANSPARENCY AND ENGAGEMENT

Creating a culture of transparency and engagement within the community is essential for building trust, reducing conflicts, and ensuring that residents feel valued and involved. Here's how to foster this culture through effective communication:

1. **Promote Open Communication:**

    Encourage open communication between residents, board members, and management. This means being transparent about decisions, actively seeking feedback, and making it easy for residents to voice their concerns or suggestions.

    - **Open Forums:** Hold regular open forums or town hall meetings where residents can ask questions, share concerns, and provide input on community matters. These meetings provide a platform for open dialogue and help build a sense of community.

    - **Feedback Channels:** Provide multiple channels for residents to provide feedback, such as suggestion boxes, online forms, or direct emails. Actively encourage residents to share their thoughts and make it clear that their feedback is valued.

- **Transparency in Decision-Making:** Be transparent about the decision-making process by explaining how decisions are made, who is involved, and what factors are considered. Share meeting minutes, financial reports, and other relevant documents with residents to keep them informed.

2. **Encourage Resident Participation:**

    Active participation from residents is key to creating an engaged community. Encourage residents to get involved in community activities, serve on committees, and participate in decision-making.

    - **Volunteer Opportunities:** Create volunteer opportunities for residents, such as joining a landscaping committee, organizing events, or helping with community projects. Volunteering gives residents a sense of ownership and investment in the community.

    - **Resident-Led Initiatives:** Support resident-led initiatives by providing resources, guidance, and recognition. For example, if a group of residents wants to start a community garden, work with them to make it happen and highlight their efforts in the community newsletter.

    - **Recognize Contributions:** Recognize and celebrate residents who contribute to the community. Whether it's a resident who consistently helps with maintenance tasks or someone who organizes events, acknowledging their efforts fosters a positive and inclusive community culture.

3. **Build Trust Through Consistency:**

    Consistency in communication and actions is key to building trust within the community. When residents know what to expect and see that management follows through on promises, they are more likely to trust the leadership.

- **Follow Through on Commitments:** If you make a commitment to a resident or the board, follow through on it. Whether it's addressing a maintenance issue or implementing a new policy, delivering on promises builds trust and credibility.
- **Consistency in Enforcement:** Apply community rules and policies consistently and fairly. Residents are more likely to trust management if they see that rules are enforced uniformly and without favoritism.
- **Transparent Communication:** Be transparent about challenges or delays that may arise. For example, if a maintenance project is delayed, explain the reasons for the delay and provide an updated timeline. Transparency in communication helps manage expectations and maintains trust.

CASE STUDY: FOSTERING TRANSPARENCY AND ENGAGEMENT

David, a community manager for a large homeowners association, noticed that residents were becoming increasingly disengaged and frustrated with the lack of transparency in decision-making. To address this, David implemented several initiatives to foster a culture of transparency and engagement:

- **Open Forums:** David introduced quarterly open forums where residents could ask questions and share their concerns directly with the board and management. These forums provided a platform for open dialogue and helped residents feel more involved in the community.
- **Transparency in Financial Reporting:** David worked with the board to improve transparency in financial reporting. He provided detailed financial reports at every board meeting and

made them available to residents through the community website. This transparency helped build trust and reassured residents that their assessments were being used responsibly.

- **Resident Participation:** David encouraged residents to get involved in the community by joining committees and volunteering for projects. He recognized and celebrated the contributions of volunteers in the community newsletter, which motivated more residents to participate.

- **Consistent Communication:** David ensured that all communication with residents was consistent and transparent. He provided regular updates on ongoing projects, explained the decision-making process, and addressed any challenges openly.

As a result of these efforts, resident engagement increased, and the overall atmosphere in the community improved. Residents felt more connected to the community and trusted that management was working in their best interests.

CONCLUSION

Mastering communication is essential for successful community management. By understanding the importance of clear and consistent communication, utilizing a variety of communication channels, and applying techniques such as active listening, you can effectively engage with residents, board members, vendors, and contractors.

Handling difficult conversations with tact and leveraging technology to enhance communication are also key skills that will help you navigate the complexities of community management. Finally, fostering a culture of transparency and engagement within the community is crucial for building trust, reducing conflicts, and ensuring that all stakeholders feel valued and involved.

As you continue to develop your communication skills, remember that effective communication is not just about conveying information; it's about building relationships, understanding others, and creating a positive and inclusive community environment. By applying the principles and strategies discussed in this chapter, you'll be well-equipped to master communication in community management and lead your community to success.

CHAPTER 6

TRUSTING AND COLLABORATING WITH PROFESSIONALS

Community association management is a multifaceted role that involves more than just overseeing daily operations and addressing resident concerns. To ensure that a community runs smoothly, managers must collaborate with a wide range of professionals, including legal advisors, accountants, maintenance personnel, contractors, and vendors. These professionals provide the expertise and services necessary to maintain the community's infrastructure, finances, and legal compliance.

For someone new to the community association industry, understanding how to select, trust, and collaborate with these professionals is crucial. This chapter will guide you through the process of identifying the right experts, building and maintaining trust, and ensuring that the services provided meet the community's standards. Through case studies and practical advice, you'll learn how to manage contracts, set expectations, and foster strong professional relationships that benefit the entire community.

THE IMPORTANCE OF TRUSTING AND COLLABORATING WITH PROFESSIONALS

Building a network of trusted professionals is essential for effective community management. Whether it's a lawyer providing legal counsel, an accountant handling the association's finances, or a contractor performing maintenance work, the quality of these professionals' services directly impacts the community's well-being.

1. **Expertise and Knowledge:**

   Community managers are expected to have a broad understanding of various aspects of property management, but they cannot be experts in every field. This is where collaborating with professionals comes into play. Legal advisors, accountants, and contractors bring specialized knowledge that is crucial for making informed decisions and ensuring that the community complies with legal and regulatory requirements.

   • **Legal Advisors:** Legal professionals provide guidance on issues such as contract law, compliance with state and federal regulations, and dispute resolution. Their expertise helps prevent legal problems and ensures that the community operates within the law.

   • **Accountants:** Financial professionals manage the association's budget, handle accounting tasks, and ensure that the community's finances are in order. They provide critical insights into financial planning, tax compliance, and audit preparation.

   • **Contractors and Maintenance Personnel:** These professionals are responsible for maintaining the physical aspects of the community, from landscaping to structural repairs. Their work ensures that the property remains safe, functional, and aesthetically pleasing.

2. **Building Trust:**

   Trust is the foundation of any successful professional relationship. When you trust the professionals you work with, you can delegate tasks with confidence, knowing that they will be handled competently and ethically. Building trust involves selecting the right professionals, communicating openly, and fostering a collaborative environment.

- **Selection Process:** Choosing the right professionals is the first step in building trust. This involves conducting thorough vetting, checking references, and assessing the professional's reputation and experience.

- **Open Communication:** Regular communication is key to maintaining trust. By keeping professionals informed about the community's needs and expectations, and by being transparent about challenges and concerns, you build a relationship based on mutual respect and understanding.

- **Accountability:** Holding professionals accountable for their work is essential for maintaining trust. This means setting clear expectations, monitoring performance, and addressing any issues promptly and fairly.

3. **Collaboration for Success:**

   Effective collaboration with professionals leads to better outcomes for the community. By working together, managers and professionals can leverage each other's strengths, share knowledge, and develop solutions that meet the community's needs.

   - **Strategic Partnerships:** Viewing your relationship with professionals as a partnership rather than a transaction fosters collaboration. Strategic partnerships involve mutual goal-setting, shared responsibility, and a focus on long-term success.

   - **Continuous Improvement:** Collaboration allows for continuous improvement. By regularly reviewing the performance of professionals and providing constructive feedback, you can ensure that the services provided evolve to meet the community's changing needs.

- **Problem-Solving:** When issues arise, collaboration enables more effective problem-solving. Professionals bring their expertise to the table, while managers provide insights into the community's specific needs and preferences. Together, you can develop solutions that are both practical and effective.

SELECTING THE RIGHT PROFESSIONALS

Choosing the right professionals to work with is critical to the success of your community management efforts. The selection process involves careful consideration of the professional's qualifications, experience, reputation, and alignment with the community's values and goals.

1. **Legal Advisors:**

    Legal advisors play a crucial role in community association management by providing guidance on a wide range of legal issues, from contract negotiations to compliance with local, state, and federal regulations. Selecting the right legal advisor requires a thorough understanding of your community's legal needs.

    - **Specialization:** Choose a legal advisor who specializes in community association law. This area of law has unique aspects that require specialized knowledge, such as understanding governing documents, fair housing laws, and dispute resolution procedures.

    - **Experience:** Look for a legal advisor with experience working with communities similar to yours. An attorney who has successfully handled cases or provided counsel to similar associations will be better equipped to address your community's specific legal challenges.

    - **Reputation:** Check the advisor's reputation by asking for references and reading reviews. Speak with other community managers or board members who have worked with the attorney to get a sense of their professionalism, responsiveness, and effectiveness.

- **Compatibility:** Ensure that the legal advisor's communication style and approach align with your community's values and expectations. A good fit between the attorney and the board is essential for a productive working relationship.

2. **Accountants:**

Accountants are responsible for managing the community's finances, which is one of the most critical aspects of community management. The right accountant will not only handle day-to-day accounting tasks but also provide strategic financial advice that supports the community's long-term goals.

- **Qualifications:** Choose an accountant with relevant qualifications, such as a Certified Public Accountant (CPA) designation. This ensures that they have met the rigorous educational and professional standards required to provide high-quality financial services.

- **Experience:** Look for an accountant with experience in community association management. Managing the finances of a homeowners association (HOA) or condominium association requires specific knowledge of budgeting, assessments, reserves, and audits.

- **Trustworthiness:** Financial transparency and integrity are paramount when selecting an accountant. Ensure that the accountant has a strong track record of ethical conduct and that they provide clear, accurate, and timely financial reports.

- **Communication Skills:** The accountant should be able to explain financial matters in a way that is understandable to board members and residents, who may not have a financial background. Clear communication helps build trust and ensures that everyone is on the same page.

3. **Contractors and Maintenance Personnel:**

Contractors and maintenance personnel are responsible for the physical upkeep of the community. Whether it's routine maintenance, landscaping, or major repairs, the quality of their work directly impacts the community's safety, appearance, and property values.

- **Licensing and Insurance:** Ensure that contractors and maintenance personnel are properly licensed and insured. This protects the community from liability and ensures that the work is performed to industry standards.

- **References and Past Work:** Ask for references and review examples of past work. A contractor with a proven track record of quality work in similar communities is more likely to meet your expectations.

- **Clear Scope of Work:** Clearly define the scope of work in the contract, including specific tasks, timelines, materials, and payment terms. This reduces the risk of misunderstandings and ensures that both parties have a clear understanding of what is expected.

- **Ongoing Monitoring:** Even after selecting a contractor, it's important to monitor their work to ensure it meets the community's standards. Regular inspections and progress meetings can help identify any issues early on and keep the project on track.

CASE STUDY: SELECTING THE RIGHT CONTRACTOR

Consider a scenario where a community manager named Alex was tasked with overseeing a major renovation project for a large condominium association. The project involved replacing the roofs on several buildings, a task that required a reliable and experienced contractor.

- **Selection Process:** Alex began by researching contractors with experience in similar projects. He checked references, reviewed past projects, and verified that the contractors were properly licensed and insured.

- **Interviews:** Alex conducted interviews with several contractors to assess their communication skills, approach to the project, and compatibility with the board's expectations. He looked for contractors who were not only technically skilled but also good communicators who could work collaboratively with the board and residents.

- **Clear Contract:** After selecting a contractor, Alex worked with the legal advisor to draft a detailed contract that outlined the scope of work, payment schedule, and project timeline. The contract also included clauses for resolving disputes and addressing any delays.

- **Ongoing Monitoring:** Throughout the project, Alex conducted regular site visits and held progress meetings with the contractor to ensure that the work was being completed according to the agreed-upon standards. When an issue with the supply of materials arose, Alex and the contractor worked together to find a solution that minimized delays.

The project was completed on time and within budget, thanks to Alex's careful selection process and ongoing collaboration with the contractor. The quality of the work was excellent, and the residents were satisfied with the outcome.

BUILDING AND MAINTAINING TRUST WITH PROFESSIONALS

Once you've selected the right professionals, the next step is to build and maintain a trusting relationship with them. Trust is built over time through consistent, transparent, and ethical interactions.

1. **Setting Clear Expectations:**

    Setting clear expectations from the outset is crucial for building trust. This involves outlining the scope of work, timelines, quality standards, and communication protocols.

    •   **Detailed Contracts:** Use detailed contracts that clearly define the responsibilities of each party. The contract should include the scope of work, deadlines, payment terms, and any specific requirements or standards that must be met.

    •   **Performance Metrics:** Establish performance metrics that will be used to evaluate the quality of the work. These metrics should be objective and measurable, such as adherence to timelines, quality of materials, and responsiveness to issues.

    •   **Regular Communication:** Set up regular communication channels, such as weekly progress meetings or status reports, to keep everyone informed about the project's progress. This ensures that any issues can be addressed promptly and prevents misunderstandings.

2. **Fostering Open and Transparent Communication:**

    Open and transparent communication is key to maintaining trust. This means being honest about challenges, providing regular updates, and being receptive to feedback.

    •   **Regular Updates:** Keep professionals informed about any changes or developments that may affect their work. This includes changes in the community's needs, budget adjustments, or new priorities from the board.

- **Feedback and Adjustments:** Provide constructive feedback on the professionals' performance and be open to receiving feedback from them as well. If there are areas for improvement, discuss them openly and work together to make the necessary adjustments.
- **Transparency in Decision-Making:** Involve professionals in the decision-making process when their expertise is required. For example, if a legal issue arises, consult with your legal advisor before making any decisions. This shows that you value their input and builds a collaborative relationship.

3. **Holding Professionals Accountable:**

Accountability is essential for maintaining trust. It ensures that professionals deliver on their promises and that any issues are addressed promptly and fairly.

- **Regular Monitoring:** Monitor the performance of professionals regularly to ensure that they are meeting the agreed-upon standards. This can include site visits, progress meetings, and reviewing reports.
- **Addressing Issues Promptly:** If an issue arises, address it promptly and directly with the professional involved. Use the contract as a reference point to discuss any discrepancies between expectations and performance.
- **Fair Resolution:** When resolving issues, aim for a fair outcome that respects the interests of both the community and the professional. This might involve renegotiating terms, adjusting timelines, or finding alternative solutions.

4. **Building Long-Term Relationships:**

Long-term relationships with trusted professionals can lead to more efficient and effective management of the community.

Over time, these professionals become familiar with the community's needs and can provide more tailored services.

- **Consistency:** Working with the same professionals over time allows for consistency in service delivery. Professionals who are familiar with the community's history, culture, and preferences can provide more effective and proactive solutions.
- **Loyalty and Trust:** Long-term relationships build loyalty and trust. Professionals who feel valued and respected are more likely to go the extra mile to meet the community's needs and resolve issues quickly.
- **Collaboration and Innovation:** Over time, long-term relationships foster collaboration and innovation. Professionals who have a deep understanding of the community can suggest new ideas, improvements, or cost-saving measures that benefit the community.

CASE STUDY: BUILDING A LONG-TERM RELATIONSHIP WITH AN ACCOUNTANT

Maria, a community manager for a mid-sized homeowners association, recognized the importance of having a trusted accountant to manage the community's finances. She selected an accountant with a strong reputation and experience in community association management.

- **Setting Expectations:** Maria and the accountant worked together to establish clear expectations for financial reporting, budgeting, and audit preparation. They agreed on a schedule for regular financial reviews and set up a system for tracking expenses and income.
- **Open Communication:** Maria maintained open communication with the accountant, providing regular updates on the

community's financial needs and any changes in the budget. The accountant, in turn, provided detailed financial reports and was always available to answer questions or provide advice.

- **Accountability:** Maria regularly reviewed the accountant's performance, ensuring that financial reports were accurate, timely, and aligned with the community's goals. When a minor discrepancy was found in the budget, Maria and the accountant worked together to resolve it quickly.

- **Long-Term Collaboration:** Over the years, Maria and the accountant developed a strong working relationship based on trust and mutual respect. The accountant's deep understanding of the community's finances allowed him to provide strategic advice that helped the association save money and plan for future projects.

The long-term relationship between Maria and the accountant resulted in a stable and well-managed financial situation for the community, with residents and board members alike expressing confidence in the association's financial health.

MANAGING CONTRACTS AND SERVICE DELIVERY

Managing contracts effectively is a key aspect of collaborating with professionals. A well-drafted contract sets the foundation for a successful working relationship by clearly defining the terms, expectations, and responsibilities of each party.

1. **Drafting and Reviewing Contracts:**

    Contracts should be comprehensive and clear, covering all aspects of the service or work to be performed. It's important to work with your legal advisor to draft and review contracts to ensure that they are legally sound and protect the community's interests.

- **Scope of Work:** The contract should clearly define the scope of work, including specific tasks, deliverables, timelines, and quality standards. This ensures that both parties have a clear understanding of what is expected.
- **Payment Terms:** Outline the payment terms, including the total cost, payment schedule, and any conditions for payment. Specify whether payments are tied to the completion of certain milestones or deliverables.
- **Termination Clauses:** Include clauses that outline the conditions under which the contract can be terminated by either party. This provides a clear process for ending the contract if the professional fails to meet expectations.
- **Dispute Resolution:** Include a dispute resolution clause that outlines the process for resolving any disagreements that may arise during the course of the contract. This could include mediation, arbitration, or legal action.

2. **Setting Performance Standards:**

   Performance standards are essential for ensuring that the work meets the community's expectations. These standards should be objective, measurable, and clearly outlined in the contract.

   - **Quality of Work:** Specify the quality standards that the work must meet. This could include materials used, craftsmanship, and adherence to industry best practices.
   - **Timeliness:** Set clear deadlines for the completion of tasks or milestones. Include penalties for delays, if applicable, to incentivize timely completion.
   - **Responsiveness:** Define expectations for communication and responsiveness. For example, the contract might specify that the professional must respond to emails or phone calls within a certain timeframe.

3. **Monitoring and Evaluating Performance:**

    Monitoring the performance of professionals is crucial for ensuring that the work is progressing as planned and meets the agreed-upon standards. Regular evaluations help identify any issues early on and allow for adjustments to be made.

    -   **Site Visits and Inspections:** Conduct regular site visits and inspections to monitor the progress of the work. This is especially important for large projects or ongoing maintenance work.

    -   **Progress Reports:** Request regular progress reports from the professional, detailing the work completed, any challenges encountered, and the next steps. This keeps you informed and allows you to address any issues promptly.

    -   **Performance Reviews:** At the end of the contract, conduct a performance review to evaluate the quality of the work and the professional's overall performance. Use this review to decide whether to continue the relationship or seek other options in the future.

4. **Ensuring Quality Service Delivery:**

    Ensuring quality service delivery requires a proactive approach to managing professionals and addressing any issues that arise. By setting clear expectations, monitoring progress, and providing feedback, you can ensure that the work meets the community's standards.

    -   **Clear Communication:** Maintain clear and open communication throughout the project. Keep professionals informed of any changes or new expectations, and encourage them to do the same.

- **Addressing Issues:** If issues arise, address them promptly and directly. Use the contract as a reference to discuss any discrepancies between expectations and performance.

- **Continuous Improvement:** Encourage professionals to continuously improve their services. Provide constructive feedback and recognize their efforts when they go above and beyond.

CASE STUDY: MANAGING A LANDSCAPING CONTRACT

John, a community manager for a large gated community, was responsible for managing a landscaping contract that involved maintaining the community's common areas, including lawns, gardens, and walking paths.

- **Contract Drafting:** John worked with the legal advisor to draft a detailed contract that outlined the scope of work, including specific tasks such as mowing, trimming, and seasonal planting. The contract also included performance standards, such as the frequency of maintenance and the quality of materials used.

- **Performance Standards:** The contract set clear performance standards, including timelines for completing tasks and expectations for the appearance of the landscaped areas. John also included a clause for regular site inspections to ensure that the work met the community's standards.

- **Monitoring Progress:** John conducted regular site visits to monitor the landscaping work and held monthly progress meetings with the contractor. He also requested weekly progress reports that detailed the work completed and any challenges encountered.

- **Addressing Issues:** When John noticed that the lawns were not being mowed as frequently as agreed upon, he addressed the issue with the contractor immediately. They discussed the importance of adhering to the maintenance schedule, and the contractor adjusted their staffing to meet the expectations.

- **Quality Service Delivery:** By setting clear expectations, monitoring progress, and addressing issues promptly, John ensured that the landscaping work was completed to the community's satisfaction. The common areas remained well-maintained, and residents expressed their appreciation for the quality of the landscaping.

SUCCESSFUL COLLABORATION: CASE STUDIES AND LESSONS LEARNED

Successful collaboration with professionals can lead to significant improvements in community management, from enhancing the quality of services to resolving complex issues. The following case studies highlight examples of successful partnerships and the lessons learned from these experiences.

Case Study 1: Legal Advisor Resolves a Dispute

A homeowners association (HOA) faced a legal dispute with a neighboring property owner over the use of a shared driveway. The property owner claimed that the HOA was infringing on their property rights, leading to a tense situation that threatened to escalate into a lawsuit.

- **Selecting the Right Legal Advisor:** The community manager, Claire, selected a legal advisor with experience in property disputes and community association law. The attorney had a strong reputation for resolving conflicts through negotiation rather than litigation.

- **Collaborative Approach:** Claire and the legal advisor worked closely together to gather all relevant information, including property records, easement agreements, and communication with the property owner. They developed a strategy that focused on finding a mutually beneficial solution.

- **Negotiation and Resolution:** The legal advisor initiated negotiations with the property owner's attorney, emphasizing the importance of maintaining a positive relationship between the two parties. Through collaborative discussions, they reached an agreement that allowed for shared use of the driveway while respecting the property owner's rights.

- **Outcome:** The dispute was resolved without the need for litigation, saving the HOA significant legal costs and preserving the relationship with the neighboring property owner. The success of the collaboration was attributed to the careful selection of the legal advisor and the strategic approach to negotiation.

- **Lesson Learned:** Selecting the right professional and taking a collaborative approach to problem-solving can lead to positive outcomes, even in challenging situations. Trust and communication are key to successful collaboration.

Case Study 2: Accountant Helps Improve Financial Health

A condominium association was struggling with budget deficits and financial mismanagement. The community's reserves were depleted, and residents were concerned about the long-term financial health of the association.

- **Selecting a New Accountant:** The community manager, Kevin, decided to hire a new accountant with experience in turning around financially troubled associations. He selected an accountant with a CPA designation and a strong track record of improving financial management in similar communities.

- **Setting Clear Expectations:** Kevin and the accountant established clear expectations for financial reporting, budgeting, and audit preparation. They also developed a plan to rebuild the association's reserves and reduce expenses.

- **Transparency and Communication:** The accountant provided detailed financial reports to the board and residents, explaining the current financial situation and the steps being taken to improve it. Kevin ensured that the communication was transparent and that residents were kept informed of the progress.

- **Outcome:** Within a year, the association's financial health had improved significantly. The reserves were rebuilt, expenses were reduced, and the budget was balanced. Residents expressed confidence in the association's financial management, and the board was able to plan for future projects with greater certainty.

- **Lesson Learned:** A skilled and experienced professional can make a significant difference in the financial health of a community. Transparency, clear communication, and setting realistic goals are essential for successful financial management.

Case Study 3: Contractor Partnership Enhances Community Amenities

A homeowners association wanted to upgrade its community amenities, including the clubhouse, pool, and playground. The project was complex and required coordination with multiple contractors, including builders, electricians, and landscapers.

- **Selecting the Right Contractors:** The community manager, Emily, carefully selected contractors with experience in similar projects. She checked references, reviewed past work, and ensured that all contractors were properly licensed and insured.

- **Collaborative Planning:** Emily organized a series of planning meetings with all the contractors involved to ensure that everyone was aligned on the project's goals, timelines, and quality standards. She emphasized the importance of collaboration and open communication throughout the project.

- **Regular Monitoring:** Emily conducted regular site visits and held weekly progress meetings with the contractors to monitor the work. She addressed any issues promptly and worked with the contractors to find solutions that kept the project on track.

- **Outcome:** The project was completed on time and within budget, and the upgraded amenities exceeded residents' expectations. The contractors appreciated Emily's collaborative approach, and the community benefited from the high-quality work.

- **Lesson Learned:** Successful collaboration with multiple professionals requires careful planning, clear communication, and regular monitoring. By fostering a collaborative environment, you can ensure that complex projects are completed successfully.

CONCLUSION

Trusting and collaborating with professionals is a fundamental aspect of effective community management. From selecting the right experts to building and maintaining strong relationships, your ability to work with legal advisors, accountants, contractors, and other professionals directly impacts the success of your community.

Throughout this chapter, we've explored the importance of trust, the process of selecting the right professionals, and strategies for managing contracts and ensuring quality service delivery. The case studies provided real-world examples of successful collaborations and the positive outcomes they can achieve.

As you continue your journey in community association management, remember that your success is closely tied to the professionals you work with. By building trust, fostering collaboration, and maintaining open communication, you can create a network of trusted partners who support the community's goals and contribute to its long-term success.

CHAPTER 7

PATH TO EFFECTIVE MANAGEMENT

As we come to the end of this comprehensive guide on community association management, it's essential to take a step back and reflect on the key themes and lessons covered throughout the chapters. The journey you've embarked on—from understanding the fundamentals of community management to mastering communication, building professional relationships, and continuous development—forms the backbone of effective management in this field.

This concluding chapter is designed to reinforce the invaluable insights you've gained and to provide a cohesive roadmap that integrates all the strategies and tools discussed. Whether you're a current manager looking to refine your skills or an aspiring manager eager to make your mark, this final chapter will empower you to excel in your role and create thriving, well-managed communities.

REVISITING THE CORE THEMES OF COMMUNITY MANAGEMENT

Throughout the book, several core themes have emerged as essential pillars of effective community management. Let's revisit these themes and explore how they interconnect to form a holistic approach to managing community associations.

1. **Holistic Understanding of Community Management**
    At the heart of successful community management lies a comprehensive understanding of the multifaceted nature of the

role. Community managers must navigate a wide range of responsibilities, from governance and financial oversight to maintenance and resident relations. This holistic understanding is the foundation upon which all other skills and strategies are built.

- **Governance:** Understanding the legal and regulatory framework that governs community associations is critical. Managers must ensure compliance with state and federal laws, as well as the association's governing documents. This involves working closely with the board of directors to implement policies, enforce rules, and make informed decisions that benefit the community as a whole.

- **Financial Oversight:** Effective financial management is crucial for the long-term sustainability of any community. Managers must be proficient in budgeting, financial planning, and reserve management. This includes working with accountants to ensure that the association's finances are transparent, well-managed, and aligned with the community's goals.

- **Maintenance and Operations:** The physical upkeep of the community is a core responsibility of the manager. This involves coordinating with contractors and maintenance personnel to ensure that common areas are well-maintained, safety standards are met, and necessary repairs are completed in a timely manner.

- **Resident Relations:** Building positive relationships with residents is key to creating a harmonious community. This requires strong communication skills, the ability to resolve conflicts, and a commitment to fostering a sense of community among residents.

By integrating these elements into your management approach, you can develop a comprehensive strategy that addresses all aspects of community management, leading to a well-rounded and effective leadership style.

2. **The Role of Continuous Professional Development**

Continuous professional development is another central theme that has been emphasized throughout this book. In an industry that is constantly evolving, staying current with the latest trends, regulations, and best practices is essential for maintaining your effectiveness as a community manager.

- **Pursuing Professional Credentials:** Earning certifications such as CMCA, AMS, PCAM, and others not only enhances your knowledge and skills but also demonstrates your commitment to professionalism. These credentials provide you with the tools and expertise needed to excel in your role and advance your career.

- **Lifelong Learning:** Beyond certifications, continuous learning involves staying informed about industry developments, attending conferences, participating in webinars, and reading relevant publications. Engaging with ongoing education opportunities helps you stay ahead of the curve and adapt to changes in the industry.

- **Networking and Mentorship:** Building a network of peers, mentors, and industry professionals is invaluable for your professional growth. Networking provides opportunities to share experiences, learn from others, and gain insights into best practices. Mentorship, in particular, offers guidance and support from more experienced managers, helping you navigate challenges and develop your leadership skills.

- **Embracing Innovation:** The community management industry is increasingly leveraging technology to improve efficiency and enhance communication. Staying open to new tools and technologies, such as community management software, virtual meeting platforms, and digital communication channels, can help you streamline operations and provide better service to your community.

    By committing to continuous professional development, you position yourself as a knowledgeable and adaptable leader who is well-equipped to meet the evolving needs of your community.

3. **The Importance of Strong, Collaborative Relationships**

    Collaboration is a recurring theme in effective community management, encompassing relationships with the board of directors, residents, and a wide range of professionals. Strong, collaborative relationships are the glue that holds a well-managed community together.

    - **Working with the Board of Directors:** The board of directors plays a pivotal role in the governance of the community. Building a strong partnership with the board is essential for implementing policies, making decisions, and resolving issues. This involves clear communication, mutual respect, and a shared commitment to the community's goals.

    - **Engaging with Residents:** Resident engagement is key to fostering a positive community atmosphere. By actively listening to residents, addressing their concerns, and encouraging participation in community activities, you can build trust and create a sense of belonging among residents.

    - **Collaborating with Professionals:** Managing a community association requires the support of various professionals, including legal advisors, accountants, contractors, and vendors. Building trust and maintaining strong relationships with these professionals ensures that the services provided are of high quality and aligned with the community's needs.

- **Conflict Resolution:** Collaboration also involves effectively managing conflicts that arise within the community. Whether it's a dispute between residents or a disagreement with a vendor, the ability to mediate and find mutually beneficial solutions is crucial for maintaining harmony and ensuring the smooth operation of the community.

By fostering strong, collaborative relationships, you create a supportive and cooperative environment that enhances the overall success of the community.

INTEGRATING STRATEGIES AND TOOLS FOR EFFECTIVE MANAGEMENT

Throughout the book, we've discussed various strategies and tools that can help you become a more effective community manager. In this section, we'll integrate these strategies into a cohesive approach that you can apply to your daily management tasks.

1. **Communication Strategies**

   Effective communication is the cornerstone of successful community management. Whether you're communicating with residents, board members, or professionals, the strategies you use can significantly impact the outcome of your interactions.

   - **Clarity and Consistency:** Ensure that your communication is clear and consistent across all channels. This helps prevent misunderstandings and ensures that all stakeholders are well-informed.
   - **Active Listening:** Practice active listening by fully engaging with the speaker, reflecting on their concerns, and

responding thoughtfully. This builds trust and fosters positive relationships.

- **Handling Difficult Conversations:** Approach difficult conversations with tact and empathy. Prepare in advance, be honest and direct, and focus on finding solutions that address the underlying issues.

- **Leveraging Technology:** Use technology to enhance communication within the community. Digital tools such as email, community websites, and social media platforms can help you reach a wider audience and provide real-time updates.

By mastering these communication strategies, you can effectively convey information, resolve conflicts, and build strong relationships with all stakeholders.

2. **Financial Management Tools**

Financial management is a critical aspect of community association management. The tools and strategies you use to manage the community's finances can have a significant impact on its long-term sustainability.

- **Budgeting and Planning:** Develop a comprehensive budget that accounts for both short-term and long-term expenses. Regularly review and adjust the budget to reflect changes in the community's needs and priorities.

- **Reserve Management:** Ensure that the association maintains adequate reserves for future capital improvements and unexpected expenses. Work with your accountant to develop a reserve study and plan for future expenditures.

- **Financial Reporting:** Provide transparent and accurate financial reports to the board and residents. This includes regular updates on income, expenses, and reserve balances.

Clear reporting builds trust and ensures that all stakeholders are informed about the community's financial health.

- **Cost Control:** Implement strategies for controlling costs and optimizing spending. This might include negotiating better contracts with vendors, reducing unnecessary expenses, or finding more cost-effective solutions for maintenance and repairs.

By applying these financial management tools, you can ensure that the community's finances are well-managed and aligned with its long-term goals.

3. **Professional Collaboration Techniques**

   Collaborating effectively with professionals is essential for maintaining the community's infrastructure, legal compliance, and financial health. The techniques you use to manage these relationships can lead to better outcomes and a more smoothly run community.

   - **Selecting the Right Professionals:** Carefully vet and select professionals who have the expertise, experience, and reputation to meet the community's needs. This includes legal advisors, accountants, contractors, and vendors.

   - **Building Trust:** Establish trust with professionals by setting clear expectations, communicating openly, and holding them accountable for their work. Trust is the foundation of a successful professional relationship.

   - **Contract Management:** Draft and review contracts carefully to ensure that they protect the community's interests and clearly define the responsibilities of each party. Include clauses for performance standards, timelines, and dispute resolution.

- **Continuous Improvement:** Regularly evaluate the performance of professionals and provide constructive feedback. Encourage continuous improvement and innovation to ensure that the services provided remain aligned with the community's evolving needs.

By mastering these professional collaboration techniques, you can build strong partnerships that contribute to the overall success of the community.

4. **Resident Engagement Strategies**

Engaging residents is key to creating a positive community atmosphere and ensuring that residents feel valued and included. The strategies you use to engage residents can significantly impact their satisfaction and participation in community activities.

- **Open Communication:** Maintain open lines of communication with residents, providing regular updates on community operations, upcoming events, and important decisions. This helps build trust and keeps residents informed.

- **Feedback Mechanisms:** Provide multiple channels for residents to provide feedback, such as surveys, suggestion boxes, and open forums. Actively seek out and consider resident input when making decisions.

- **Community Building Activities:** Organize events and activities that bring residents together and foster a sense of community. This might include social events, volunteer opportunities, or workshops.

- **Conflict Resolution:** Address resident concerns and conflicts promptly and fairly. Use mediation and active listening to find solutions that satisfy all parties involved.

By implementing these resident engagement strategies, you can create a supportive and inclusive community where residents feel connected and valued.

5. **Governance and Leadership**

   Effective governance and leadership are essential for guiding the community toward its goals and ensuring that it operates smoothly and in compliance with legal and regulatory requirements.

   - **Working with the Board:** Build a strong partnership with the board of directors by providing guidance, support, and expertise. Help the board make informed decisions that are in the best interest of the community.

   - **Policy Implementation:** Ensure that community policies are implemented fairly and consistently. This includes enforcing rules, managing compliance, and addressing violations in a way that is transparent and respectful.

   - **Vision and Planning:** Work with the board to develop a long-term vision for the community and create strategic plans to achieve that vision. This might include setting goals for infrastructure improvements, financial stability, and resident satisfaction.

   - **Ethical Leadership:** Lead by example by adhering to ethical standards and demonstrating integrity in all aspects of your work. Ethical leadership builds trust and sets a positive tone for the entire community.

   By focusing on governance and leadership, you can guide the community toward its goals and create a stable, well-managed environment for all residents.

EMPOWERING YOU TO EXCEL IN COMMUNITY MANAGEMENT

The strategies, tools, and insights discussed throughout this book are designed to empower you to excel in your role as a community association manager. Whether you're just starting out or looking to refine your skills, the knowledge you've gained provides a strong foundation for success.

1. **Developing a Personalized Management Approach**

   Every community is unique, and there is no one-size-fits-all approach to community management. Use the strategies and tools discussed in this book to develop a personalized management approach that aligns with the specific needs and goals of your community.

   - **Assessing Community Needs:** Regularly assess the needs and priorities of your community. This might involve conducting surveys, holding town hall meetings, or working with the board to identify key areas for improvement.

   - **Adapting Strategies:** Be flexible and willing to adapt your strategies as the community evolves. What works for one community may not work for another, so it's important to tailor your approach to the specific context.

   - **Continuous Improvement:** Commit to continuous improvement by regularly reviewing your performance and seeking out opportunities for growth. This might include pursuing additional certifications, learning new skills, or seeking feedback from residents and board members.

2. **Fostering a Culture of Excellence**

   Creating a culture of excellence within the community is key to achieving long-term success. This involves setting high standards, encouraging collaboration, and celebrating achievements.

- **Setting High Standards:** Set high standards for yourself, the board, and the professionals you work with. Strive for excellence in all aspects of community management, from financial oversight to resident relations.
- **Encouraging Collaboration:** Foster a collaborative environment where board members, residents, and professionals work together toward common goals. Encourage open communication, mutual respect, and shared responsibility.
- **Celebrating Achievements:** Recognize and celebrate the achievements of the community, whether it's completing a major project, improving resident satisfaction, or achieving financial stability. Celebrating successes helps build morale and motivates everyone to continue striving for excellence.

3. **Embracing Your Role as a Leader**

    As a community association manager, you play a vital role in shaping the future of your community. Embrace your role as a leader by demonstrating integrity, building trust, and guiding the community toward its goals.

    - **Leading with Integrity:** Integrity is the cornerstone of effective leadership. Be honest, transparent, and ethical in all your interactions. Leading with integrity builds trust and sets a positive example for the entire community.
    - **Building Trust:** Trust is earned through consistent, transparent, and ethical behavior. Work to build trust with residents, board members, and professionals by being reliable, responsive, and fair.
    - **Guiding the Community:** Use your knowledge, skills, and experience to guide the community toward its goals. This involves setting a vision, creating strategic plans, and

working collaboratively with all stakeholders to achieve success.

4. Preparing for Future Challenges

Community association management is a dynamic field that presents new challenges and opportunities every day. By staying informed, continuously improving your skills, and building strong relationships, you'll be well-prepared to navigate these challenges and lead your community to success.

- **Staying Informed:** Keep up with industry trends, regulatory changes, and emerging best practices by reading relevant publications, attending conferences, and participating in professional development opportunities.

- **Adapting to Change:** Be flexible and adaptable in the face of change. Whether it's a new regulation, a shift in resident demographics, or an unforeseen challenge, your ability to adapt and find solutions will be key to your success.

- **Anticipating Future Needs:** Proactively anticipate the future needs of your community by planning for growth, addressing potential risks, and setting long-term goals. By thinking ahead, you can ensure that your community remains resilient and well-prepared for the future.

YOUR PATH TO SUCCESS IN COMMUNITY MANAGEMENT

As you conclude this book, remember that the path to success in community management is built on a foundation of knowledge, collaboration, and continuous improvement. The insights and strategies you've gained provide the tools you need to excel in your role and create thriving, well-managed communities.

By embracing a holistic understanding of community management, committing to continuous professional development, and building strong, collaborative relationships, you'll be well-equipped to lead your community with confidence and integrity.

Your journey as a community association manager is an ongoing process of growth, learning, and leadership. As you apply the lessons from this book to your daily work, you'll not only enhance your own effectiveness but also contribute to the well-being and success of the communities you serve.

Thank you for taking the time to explore the principles and practices of effective community management. As you continue on your path, remember that your dedication, professionalism, and commitment to excellence are the keys to creating thriving, harmonious communities that residents are proud to call home.